Alfred Sanders

Contributions to the Anatomy of the Central Nervous

System in Vertebrate Animals

Alfred Sanders

**Contributions to the Anatomy of the Central Nervous System in Vertebrate
Animals**

ISBN/EAN: 9783337815127

Printed in Europe, USA, Canada, Australia, Japan

Cover: Foto ©ninafisch / pixelio.de

More available books at **www.hansebooks.com**

XXII. *Contributions to the Anatomy of the Central Nervous System in Vertebrate Animals.*

By ALFRED SANDERS, *M.R.C.S., F.L.S., late Lecturer on Comparative Anatomy at the London Hospital Medical College.*

Communicated by Professor HUXLEY, *Sec. R.S.*

Received May 7,—Read May 23, 1878.

[PLATES 58–65.]

Part I.—ICHTHYOPSIDA.   Section 1.—PISCES.   Subsection 1.—TELEOSTEI.

Introduction.

INVESTIGATIONS into the histology of the nervous system in Vertebrata, have hitherto been chiefly confined to that of the Mammalia, or if applied to the lower members of that sub-kingdom, have not been undertaken so much with reference to the morphological relationship of animals, as to their bearings on physiology and the art of medicine. It may be stated in general terms that those who have worked at the morphology of the nervous system have not paid much attention to its histology ; and, per contra, those who have investigated the histology have neglected its morphological bearing. STIEDA, however, has investigated the brain in both aspects of the question, and LOCKHART CLARKE has made some reference to the nervous system of the lower Vertebrata in his classical investigations, but this bears but a subordinate proportion to the whole. FRITSCH has recently published a treatise on the histology of the central nervous system in Fishes, in which the homology of the various parts is especially considered.

It occurred to me that the proper method of research in such complicated organs as the central nervous system, would be to proceed from the more simple to the more intricate, and I have selected the Teleostei as a good starting point in the class Pisces, as they form a sort of central group from which the other orders diverge either in a progressive or in a retrograde direction.

The species which I have more particularly investigated has been the Grey Mullet (*Mugil cephalus*), and unless the contrary is mentioned, the statements in the following pages apply to that species.

For a great part of the material used, I am indebted to the kindness of Dr. EISIG, of the zoological station at Naples, who provided me with living specimens, without which it would be impossible to obtain an accurate idea of the histological elements, since the nervous tissue deteriorates with great rapidity after death.

The method of procedure was to disable the animal by cutting through the spinal cord behind the pectoral fins, and as rapidly as possible after opening the cranium to dissect out the brain, and to place it at once in absolute alcohol, to which some drops of tincture of iodine had been added so as to give it the colour of pale sherry. This method, which was first suggested by STIEDA (58) (see bibliographical list at p. 769 of this paper), and was adopted by him in his investigations, appears to have the effect of fixing the nervous elements at the moment of molecular death.

The hardening fluid used was chromic acid; and the great point to be attended to was not to have it too strong, and to place each brain into a large quantity of liquid. The proportions used were one part of chromic acid to 800 parts of water, and the allowance for each moderate sized brain was one grain of chromic acid with its proper quantity of water; by this means it was possible to make the medulla oblongata and the tuberosities of the brain of the same degree of hardness, so that a section could be cut including both parts. A stronger solution would cause the tuberosities of the brain to become brittle before the medulla oblongata had attained sufficient firmness to be cut. By this process a brain would take from ten days to a fortnight, according to the size, to gain the proper consistence. If it happened that it was not convenient to make sections when the brains were ready, they were kept in a solution of ten grains of potash bichromate to one ounce of water, which was occasionally changed. A short stay in this solution was rather an improvement, as the bundles of nerve-fibres thus acquired a yellowish tinge, and were not so easily coloured, so that they appeared more distinct. But a longer delay in this liquid rendered the brains very brittle, unless they were soft when first put in, and made the neuroglia become too granular, thus obscuring the view of the nervous arrangements and rendering it necessary to make thinner sections.

The colouring matter employed was rosaniline, which gives the sections a beautiful blue tint, and which is decidedly better than carmine, being easier to use and showing the minute structure of the cells much more distinctly. Hœmatoxylin also has a good effect.

As confusion is often caused by applying the terms of direction used in human anatomy to the lower animals which habitually move in a different position, perhaps it would not be superfluous to remark that the terms used in this paper have reference to that position; so that, instead of "posterior," the words "dorsal," "upper," or their derivatives will be used; for "anterior," the words "ventral" or "lower;" "anterior" or "forward" will mean towards the head; "posterior" or "behind" towards the tail, instead of the meaning attached to them in anthropotomy.

Macroscopic Anatomy of the Brain.

The brain of the Teleostei when viewed from above is composed of three pairs of tuberosities placed in a series from before backwards, and one unpaired tuberosity. The homologies of these tuberosities are not yet settled. MIKLUCHO-MACLAY (62) has within the last few years proposed an arrangement differing considerably from that ordinarily received—an arrangement which was endorsed by the great authority of GEGENBAUR (67) in his 'Grundzüge der vergleichenden Anatomie,' to which I find that he still adheres in his recently published 'Grundriss.' Notwithstanding this, it appears to me that the interpretation adopted by STIEDA (58) is more likely to be correct, and that author, in a subsequent paper (64), has given a detailed argument against their opinion.

The first pair of the tuberosities in the brain of fishes may be looked upon as the homologues of the bulbi olfactorii (fig. 1, ol.). They are pear shaped, and are not (at least in *Mugil*) connected together by a transverse commissure, but are each united separately to the second pair of tuberosities, to the anterior end of which they are closely applied. In some species—as, for instance, in the members of the Cod family, and others—the lobi olfactorii are not arranged as above mentioned, but are placed immediately over the nasal sacs, and are connected to the cerebral lobes by a long commissure; in which case the latter has the appearance of occupying the most anterior part of the cranial cavity.

The second pair of tuberosities, which I will term the cerebral lobes (figs. 1 and 2, *ce.*), are more or less rounded; they vary in size in different species. In some fishes, such as the Basse (*Labrax Lupus*) and *Scorpæna Porcus*, these bodies present furrows and ridges on their surface which might be looked upon as rudimentary convolutions. They are united by a transverse commissure which is situated on their inferior edge, and nearer the posterior than the anterior end.

Many of the older writers, who having dissected only fishes of the Carp family, in which the first pair of tuberosities are situated far in advance of the remainder of the brain and outside the cranial cavity, looked upon this second pair as the lobi olfactorii. Of these, HALLER (4) considered that they subserved the function of smell together with the lobi inferiores or hypoaria; others—as CAMPER (7), EBEL (9), WEBER (17), KUHL (21), SOMMÉ (24), GOTTSCHE (34), MAYER (49), and KLAATSCH (44)—thought that they alone constituted the lobi olfactorii; while TREVIRANUS (13), who at first termed them "Riechforsatz," subsequently altered his interpretation, and in accordance with a theory which he developed at a later period termed them "Vordere Hemisphäre." PHILIPEAUX and VULPIAN (45) considered that they represented the caruncula mammillaris at the middle root of the olfactory nerve; but the latter (56) subsequently came to the conclusion that they were the hemispheres of the brain. On the other hand, SERRES (25), BÜCHNER (33), LEURET (35), and BAUDELOT (61) homologised them with the hemispheres of the brain without reserve. GIRGENSOHN (42) was not decided, but thought that they might represent the first rudiments of those bodies.

TIEDEMANN (15) was the first who compared them to the corpora striata with the hemispheres, and their commissure to the anterior commissure of the brain—an opinion which was justified when V. BAER (32) discovered that in the course of their development these tuberosities were at first hollow and contained a small tubercle at the bottom of their ventricle, which tubercle occupied the position of the corpora striata.

Of the remaining writers, HOLLARD (55), evidently unacquainted with the researches of V. BAER, confined the interpretation of these lobes to the region of the insula. To conclude the consideration of the cerebral lobes, MIKLUCHO-MACLAY (62) and FRITSCH (66) follow V. BAER; the former termed the tuberosities in question the "vorderhirn," and the latter "hemisphœria" or "stirnhirn."

The third pair of tuberosities are the largest bodies in the brain of fishes. They are hollow, and consist of the following parts : first, a thin vault of nervous substance, the " tecta loborum opticorum " of STIEDA, which may be termed for shortness "tectum." These are united together in the mid-line by a transverse commissure, and are closed in posteriorly by a tubercle closely attached to the unpaired tuberosity behind. This is the " tuberculum cordiforme " of HALLER, and is more or less developed in different families of the Teleostei.

Along the inner contiguous edges of the tecta a pair of longitudinal ridges of a somewhat triangular shape are attached, through the bases of which the beforementioned commissure runs : these form the fornix of GOTTSCHE (34), and the commissure was termed by the same author the " corpus callosum." On the floor of the ventricle formed by these vault-like structures two hemispherical swellings are placed, which being in some fishes of a somewhat curved form, were named by HALLER " tori semicirculares."

The complicated structure of these tuberosities induced many writers on this subject to look upon them as the homologues of the hemispheres of the brain ; although one would have supposed that the position of the pineal gland and the origin from them of the optic nerve would have formed an insuperable objection to this interpretation.

CAMPER (7) was the first who made any serious attempt to decipher the homologies of the brain in fishes.

These third pair of tuberosities (which for the sake of convenience will be called here the optic lobes) were for him the cerebral hemispheres ; the commissure of the tecta was the corpus callosum, and the tuberculum cordiforme homologised the corpora quadrigemina : an opinion which was also held by HALLER ; and the ventricle of the optic lobes was the third ventricle.

KUHL (21), SOMMÉ (24), CUVIER (28), and LEURET (35) followed this interpretation.

EBEL (9) thought that these lobes, combined with the unpaired ganglion behind them, were equivalent to the cerebrum.

WEBER, in his first paper (17), considered that they were the hemispheres, but subsequently (22 and 27) he termed them "sehnervenhügel," by which he probably meant no more than that they were optic lobes, without absolutely homologising them with the thalami optici.

With GOTTSCHE (34) the tuberculum cordiforme corresponded to the corpora quadrigemina, and the commissure of the tectum was the corpus callosum, as with CAMPER.

The projecting ridges on the inner contiguous edges of the tecta, he termed the fornix.

CARUS (12) was the first to discover these bodies and also applied this name to them, but more on account of their shape, and without any reference to the fornix of anthropotomy.

GOTTSCHE considered the communication between the two sides of the ventricle of the optic lobes, beneath the two ridges above-mentioned, to be the foramen of MONRO, and the tuberosity on the floor of the ventricle to be the thalamus opticus.

TREVIRANUS (13), following CAMPER, homologised these lobes with the cerebral hemispheres, the tuberculum cordiforme with the corpora quadrigemina, and the tori semicirculares with the corpora striata combined with the thalami optici. Subsequently (29) slightly changing his interpretation, he compared them to the posterior part only of the hemispheres combined with the corpora quadrigemina. Many anatomists, with better reason, considered these lobes as the equivalent of the corpora bigemina in birds; the first of these was CARUS (12), who was followed by TIEDEMANN (15), who came to this conclusion from embryological considerations.

SERRES adopted this opinion on account of the position of the pineal gland and of the origin of the nervus patheticus, which, as he remarked, invariably arises between the corpora quadrigemina and the cerebellum.

This author refuted the objection that these bodies in the higher Vertebrata are solid, whereas in fishes they are hollow ; by the assertion, that in the embryo of those higher Vertebrata they have a cavity in them as in the Teleostei.

GIRGENSOHN (42), BAUDELOT (61), and VULPIAN (56) also follow this interpretation ; the latter having changed from his former opinion (45), in which paper he said that they were "le cerveau proprement dit."

According to V. BAER these lobes are the "zwischenhirn" (thalamencephalon), and the tuberculum cordiforme the "mittelhirn" (mesencephalon) which in some unexplained way had become thrust under the former in the process of development.

JOHANNES MÜLLER also followed this opinion ; he considered that these optic lobes were equivalent to the corpora quadrigemina conjoined to the "lobus ventriculi tertii" of the fœtus. At the point where the tecta arch over the tuberculum cordiforme, just described, there is a fissure which communicates with the ventricle of the optic lobe ; this KLAATSCH (44) considered to be the fissure of Bichat : an opinion which is obviously untenable.

The unpaired ganglion situated behind the optic lobes has almost unanimously been looked upon as the cerebellum (fig. 1, cbl., and figs. 6, 7, and 8). This tuberosity overhangs the medulla oblongata and closes in the fourth ventricle ; it varies in shape in different species, being tongue-shaped in Whiting (Merlangus vulgaris), almost square in Mugil cephalus, presents two distinct tuberosities in Labrax Lupus, and in Scorpæna Porcus is reduced to comparatively small dimensions; its anterior border is prolonged into a body (fig. 1 *v.c.*), which projects into the ventricle of the optic lobe, and was described by HALLER under the name "tuberculum cordiforme." This is essentially a prolongation of the unpaired tuberosity, which passing into the ventricle over the aquæductus sylvii, nearly as far forward as the anterior end of the same, is there turned back, and reaching the posterior and upper end of the tectum joins the so-called fornix.

In the Carp, which was the species investigated by HALLER, the lateral portions or alæ (figs. 4 and 5, *a.v.c.*) of this body are highly developed, and form several folds, the sum total of which were termed by that anatomist "cornu ammonis," probably from their form, and not as compared to the part of the same name in the human brain. This cornu ammonis is found considerably developed also in *Crenilabrus*, where it fills the whole cavity of the ventricle of the optic lobe.

It is probably the enormous development of this part which forms the extraordinary structure in the brain of *Mormyrus Cyprinoides* (Nilhecht), described by ECKER (47) and by MARCUSEN (51), and later by OEFFINGER (57). MARCUSEN thought that it was most probably the cerebellum, and MIKLUCHO-MACLAY supports that idea. As I have never had the good fortune to meet with specimens of this fish, and as the authors just mentioned do not touch upon the microscopic anatomy (except MAR-CUSEN, who does not do so very minutely), I am unable to give a decided opinion; but I should think that it was not the cerebellum precisely, with which this remarkable structure homologised, but that part of it which goes under the name of the valvula cerebelli. Of course this opinion is a mere guess, but the inspection of a few thin sections of a fresh subject would soon decide the point.

WEBER'S was one of the few exceptions to the generally received opinion that this lobe is the cerebellum; in his first paper (17) he termed it "corpus quadrigeminum seu Impar Majus," but subsequently he changed his views, and denominated it "vorderer unpaar Hügel des Kleingehirns;" while that part of the medulla oblongata which covers over the narrow part of the fourth ventricle behind it, and which in some species is developed into a distinct tuberosity, and which HALLER named "pons mammillaris," WEBER termed "Hinterer unpaar Hügel des Kleingehirns." MAYER (49) followed his opinion; his name for this part was "epicncephalon seu cerebelli lobus anterior," but he differed from WEBER in placing his "cerebelli lobus posterior" in the pair of tuberosities on the dorsal side of the medulla oblongata, from which the nervi vagi take their origin. These tuberosities are situated on the dorsal side of the medulla oblongata behind the cerebellum. They enclose between them a deep fissure, which corresponds to the posterior part of the fourth ventricle. Anteriorly in some fishes they are united together in the midline by a single tuberosity, which is situated over the narrow part of the fourth ventricle, immediately behind the crura cerebelli. Usually this tuberosity is replaced by a thin layer of granular substance occupying the same position.

MIKLUCHO-MACLAY (62) has within the last few years attempted to place the homology of the brain in fishes on a new basis firmly centred, as he supposed, on embryology. His opinion has been endorsed by no less an authority than that of GEGENBAUR (67), which even in the 'Grundriss' just published he has not seen fit to alter. The author also informs his readers that V. BAER gave to his theory a verbal assent.

This being the case, his opinion, perhaps, merits a more detailed consideration. With him, therefore, the cerebral lobes are the "vorderhirn," the optic lobes are the "zwischenhirn" (thalamencephalon), the cerebellum the "mittelhirn" (mesencephalon), and the pons mammillaris the "hinterhirn," and the posterior part of the medulla oblongata the "nachhirn." It is thus seen that the cerebellum in many fishes is reduced to a mere bridge of granular material, covering the narrow part of the fourth ventricle.

Against this scheme STIEDA (64) has placed on record several very important considerations : 1st, that the optic nerve, which in Amphibia and Birds arises from the mesencephalon (corpora quadrigemina), would, according to this mode of interpretation, arise from the thalamencephalon ; 2nd, then the trochleares would arise wrongly between the thalamencephalon and the mesencephalon ; 3rd, the thalamencephalon of fishes would not correspond to that of the amphibia, where it is a small flattened segment open above ; but in fishes, if MIKLUCHO-MACLAY be right, it becomes developed into a large closed segment, which is often paired ; 4th, the pineal gland would be wrongly placed.

With regard to the third objection, MIKLUCHO-MACLAY appears to have overlooked the real thalamencephalon, which is the territory surrounding that narrow fissure, the greater part of which is in front of the optic lobes, so that in point of fact he searched for the "zwischenhirn" too far back.

The microscopic structure of the "mittelhirn" of MIKLUCHO-MACLAY, as was also pointed out by STIEDA, and as will be seen in the following pages, so entirely corresponds to that of the cerebellum in higher Vertebrates, that any comparison of it with any other part of the brain is wholly precluded.

The brain has hitherto been considered from above. On examining its lower surface the following structures are to be observed from before backwards, viz., in front, the entrance of the optic nerve, behind which is situated the pituitary body (fig. 1, *pi.*, figs. 3 and 4) or hypophysis cerebri, placed on a slight eminence, the trigonum fissum of GOTTSCHE ; on each side a large tuberosity (fig. 1, *hy.*, figs. 3, 4, 5, and 6), the lobus inferior, or, as I think preferable, the "hypoarium," used by OWEN in his 'Anatomy of the Vertebrata:' a term having the same meaning but being less clumsy.

The posterior parts of the groove (fig. 5, *s.v.*) indicating the separation between the two hypoaria is occupied by a vascular sac, the "saccus vasculosus" or "hæmatosac." This sac in *Mugil cephalus* is not visible from the surface, being contained in a sort of chamber formed between the contiguous walls of the two hypoaria.

HALLER appears to have looked upon the hypoaria as having relation to the sense of smell, for he termed them "olfactoria inferiora" or "tubercula reniformia."

Most of the authors in the list, homologised these bodies with the corpora albicantia. CARUS (12) was the first to compare them to the tuber cinereum, with which part they agree in position. SERRES and LEURET also adopted this view, but KLAATSCH confined this interpretation to the slight eminence (the trigonum fissum) to which the hypophysis is attached. CUVIER termed them "lobes optiques;" MAYER compared them to the thalamus opticus and corpus striatum combined; while HOLLARD (55) homologised them to the corpora striata, because, as he pointed out, the fibres which correspond, as he supposed, to the corona radiata of the cerebrum pass into them to end there; but this fact was denied by VULPIAN (56), who stated that these fibres pass through them without terminating, and go on into the medulla oblongata. This, I think, is most probably an error.

GIRGENSOHN (42) emitted the curious opinion that these bodies were together a highly developed hypophysis: an opinion which is evidently based on the supposition that the latter is composed of nervous tissue. In many fishes the hypophysis is easily broken off, and does not remain attached to the brain when the latter is removed from the skull; in that case, a small fissure is seen on the trigonum from which it is torn, which is the lower opening of the infundibulum.

There is no apparent line of separation between the medulla oblongata and the spinal cord, the latter gradually passing into the former; but the posterior end of the vagal tuberosities may be taken as a landmark for want of a better.

The anterior part of the spinal cord (fig. 14) has somewhat of a four-sided figure with the angles cut off; the dorsal and the ventral fissures are represented only by shallow depressions, the dorsal one becoming deeper on approaching the posterior end of the medulla oblongata. At this part the central canal has an oval section, the long axis of which is placed at right angles to the long axis of the cord. This canal (c.ca., fig. 14) becomes smaller at a point nearer the fourth ventricle and also circular in outline; it then enlarges in a funnel-shaped manner, and becoming notched on its upper margin joins the gradually deepening dorsal fissure and enters the posterior section of the fourth ventricle. Occasionally a rod is seen in sections through this central canal of the cord, which most probably is the coagulated liquid contained therein, as STIEDA suggested; it is only in a few sections that this rod is seen, for it usually falls out, not being retained in its place by any attachments.

The fourth ventricle (fig. 10, s.r.) consists of two separate portions; the posterior part is a deep trench, situated between the two lobes of the vagus, the walls of which are nearly perpendicular and the floor rounded. Superiorly, this trench is covered by a layer of pia mater which passes over from one tuberosity to the other. Anteriorly, it passes by means of a quadrangular passage into the main part of the ventricle (fig. 9, s.r.), which is a wide space beneath the cerebellum and between the crura thereof (fig. 10). The passage between the two divisions of this ventricle is formed by a bridge of nervous tissue, which in some species* becomes enlarged into a tuberosity. Before

* Carp family.

entering the wider chamber the narrow part of the fourth ventricle becomes triangular in shape, with the base of the triangle turned upwards. The segment of this ventricle, which forms the chamber beneath the cerebellum, has the same relations that the fourth ventricle has in the human subject. It is shaped like a cocked hat when seen from above; the top of the hat being directed backwards, and the sides running out into pointed extremities; below, there is a longitudinal furrow on the floor; above, its roof at first flat afterwards becomes furrowed in the centre. There is a large triangular opening in its roof which places this ventricle in communication with the outside of the brain beneath the cerebellum; anteriorly, a lozenge-shaped passage (fig. 5, *aq.Sy.*), the aquæductus Sylvii, forms a communication between this ventricle and the ventricle of the optic lobes. Before opening into the latter the aqueduct spreads out into a wide depressed fissure. In the roof a longitudinal furrow extends from the anterior part of the fourth ventricle, and in the floor a similar furrow extends from the middle of the narrow part of the ventricle as far forward as the entrance of the aqueduct into the ventricle of the optic lobe.

With regard to this last space, GOTTSCHE (34) considered that it corresponded to the third, combined with the lateral ventricles, and FRITSCH (66) even is doubtful whether it does or does not homologise with the lateral ventricles; but I think that after all it is merely an expansion of the aquæductus Sylvii. That it does not correspond to the third ventricle appears nearly certain, since the fissure which properly corresponds to that ventricle is in front, and communicates with the space in question by a small foramen, which opens behind the posterior commissure. The third ventricle (fig. 2, *v.th.*) is situated between the two bundles of fibres which pass from the cerebral lobes into the hypoaria, and also between the two optic tracts. In front, this fissure communicates through a narrower passage with a small oblong chamber, placed close behind the anterior limits of the brain, between the bases of the two cerebral lobes, which seems to correspond to the lamina terminalis of the fœtus. The above-mentioned chamber and the narrower passage are lined by a stratum of nerve-cells; inferiorly, the third ventricle contracts into a funnel-shaped passage, the infundibulum, which leads into a space surrounded by the hypophysis, and which receives on each side the openings of the passage from the ventricles of the hypoaria.

Apparent Origin of the Cranial Nerves.

In the Teleostei, all the cranial nerves, with the exception of the hypoglossal and spinal accessory, may be distinguished, if not as separate roots, at least as divisions of some of the others. Thus, the nerve which is usually considered to be the facial is a branch of the trifacial; and the supposed glossopharyngeal is sometimes a branch of the acusticus. The four anterior nerves do not require much discussion; they arise in the same manner in all the Teleostei that I have examined.

The olfactory (fig. 1, *n.* 1), perhaps, in those fishes in which the lobe is applied close to the anterior end of the cerebral lobes may be considered as a true nerve.

The optic nerve (fig. 1, *n.* 2) is folded on itself transversely several times, so as to give its section a pectinated appearance,—a fact which was first mentioned by MALPIGHII (2).

The motores oculorum (fig. 5, *n.* 3) invariably arise from the point of junction of the hypoaria with the ventral edge of the. medulla, where a band of transverse fibres exist, which were described by GOTTSCHE under the name of " commissura ansulata ;" these nerves pass outwards, and appear in the groove between those bodies and the lower edge of the optic lobes at about the centre of their length.

The trochleares (fig. 6, *n.* 4) arise from the valvula-cerebelli, whence they pass out behind the optic lobe, and curving round the posterior edge of that body pass forward towards their destination

DESMOULINS (26) has given the origin of this nerve from the ventral surface of the medulla oblongata, where, he says, the filaments of the root of one nerve were contiguous to those of the nerve on the opposite side.   What could have induced this author to make such a mistake it is impossible to imagine.   No nerve, except the motores oculorum, and that not strictly, answers to his description ; and that nerve is precluded by the context.

The remainder of the cranial nerves vary in origin in different species of Teleostei.

The trifacial (fig. 2, *n.* 5 ; fig. 7, *n.* 5 ; fig. 8, *l.c.* 5 ; fig. 9, *l.c.* 5 and *u.c.* 5) in *Mugil cephalus* has the following arrangement : it arises by three closely contiguous roots from the side of the medulla oblongata, beneath the anterior edge of the crura cerebelli ; the casserian ganglion is developed on the middle root only ; the anterior passes forward over the ganglion, and joins the middle root in the foramen of exit, which in this species is through bone ; the posterior root passes forward to a separate foramen, through which it emerges as an independent nerve, having first received a branch from the under surface of the ganglion ; it then pursues its course obliquely through the palato-quadrate arch, and its fibres are lost on the outer surface of the quadrate bone. It is this root which is considered by anatomists to be the facial nerve.   In the *Pleuronectes*, according to STANNIUS, there are four or five roots to the trifacial, and more than one of them contribute to the formation of the facial.

The abducens (fig. 8, *n.* 6 ; fig. 9, *n.* 6) has a very constant origin ; each root arises by two small cords from the ventral surface of the medulla, beneath the anterior root of the vagus.

The acusticus arises from the medulla oblongata, on a lower level than the trifacial ; the anterior end of its root is placed exactly ventrad of the posterior root of the trifacial, while its posterior edge is in front of the anterior root of the vagus.   This nerve immediately divides into two branches : one, the anterior, goes to the anterior and horizontal semicircular canals, while the posterior goes backwards to be distributed to the sac of the otolithes ; in its course the latter gives off a small branch, which supplies the ampulla of the posterior semicircular canal.

There is a small nerve which is often merely a branch from the posterior division of the acusticus, but which in *Mugil* has a distinct origin from the medulla oblongata, immediately below the anterior root of the vagus. This nerve crosses the last-described branch of the acusticus at right angles, and passes through a distinct foramen in the outer wall of the ear sac, where it forms a moderately sized ganglion. From this ganglion two branches are given off: one supplies the anterior branchial arch; the other, passing forward in close juxtaposition to the outside of the skull, joins the posterior root of the trifacial above mentioned. This nerve is usually described as the glossopharyngeal (STANNIUS, 38, 43, BÜCHNER, 33), but WEBER (22) terms it the nervus auditorius accessorius in the Carp.

The vagus (figs. 2, 9, 10, and 11, *n*. 10) arises above the level of the acusticus and the last-mentioned nerve by two roots, the anterior of which emerging from the medulla oblongata a short distance behind the posterior edge of the crus cerebelli, passes back, and having received a communicating branch from the posterior root, emerges from the skull through a distinct foramen in the exoccipital bone. The posterior root rises opposite the posterior end of the vagal tuberosities, and after giving off the above-mentioned branch to the anterior root, passes out of the skull through a separate foramen beneath that root. Thus the two origins of the vagus do not entirely unite until they arrive at the outside of the skull in *Mugil cephalus*.

The nervus recurrens connecting the trifacial with the vagus and the so-called hypoglossal, inside the skull beneath the brain, which is described by WEBER and BÜCHNER in the Carp, is not present in this species.

In the Whiting Pollack (*Merlangus Pollachius*) all the roots of the trifacial pass through the casserian ganglion, which is placed in the course of the nerve partly within and partly without the cranial cavity.

The acusticus, as in *Mugil cephalus*, divides into two main branches, the anterior of which goes to the ampullæ of the anterior and horizontal semicircular canals, and the posterior divides into two branches; of these, the posterior joins the inferior surface of the vagus immediately beyond or at the point of junction of the two roots of that nerve; the anterior, after supplying the ampulla of the posterior semicircular canal, passes out of the cranial cavity through a foramen in the external wall of the ear cavity, where, as in *Mugil*, it developes a ganglion which is placed closed to the bone at the exit of the nerve. From this ganglion two large branches are given off: one goes back to supply the first branchial arch, the other goes forward, closely applied to the external surface of the skull, and joins the base of the casserian ganglion at a point between the branching off of the ophthalmic and the two maxillary nerves. In its course this branch supplies twigs to the anterior ends of the kidneys, and to the muscles on the inner side of the branchial arches.

This division of the acusticus is evidently the same nerve as that described in the *Mugil*, and corresponds to the glossopharyngeal of authors. It has no relation to the nervus recurrens of the Carp, which is, in point of fact, the sympathetic nerve, and remains inside the skull while the nerve in question is on the outside.

STANNIUS (38) gives an account of this nerve in the *Gadus callarias*, in which species it also developes a ganglion on the outside of the skull; but that author does not mention any connexion between it and either the acusticus (for as in the *Mugil* it has a separate origin from the brain) or the trifacial.

I would suggest that the branch of the acusticus just described homologises with the facial and not with the glossopharyngeal. From this point of view, the ganglion in the course of this nerve would be the ganglion geniculare or intumescentia, which on account of the non-development of the tympanum in Teleostei, comes to be placed outside the skull. The branch to the first branchial arch would be the twig of communication between the facial and the glossopharyngeal, and the anterior branch joining the casserian ganglion would be the auriculo temporal, or, perhaps, the main trunk. The true glossopharyngeal would be found in the branch of the vagus to be presently described.

In the evolution of the higher Vertebrate animals, when the glossopharyngeal and the facial become independent nerves, I should imagine, on the supposition that the above considerations were well founded, that the posterior branch of the ganglion in question would degenerate into the communicating twig between the facial and the glossopharyngeal; while the anterior branch would increase in size, *pari passu* with the increasing development of the muscles of the face, and at the same time become detached from immediate connexion with the trifacial.

The vagus arises here also by two roots as in *Mugil cephalus*, but they join before arriving at the foramen of exit, instead of outside the skull as in that species. The ganglion of the vagus is formed partly in the foramen, but the greater part of it is situated outside. From the upper edge of the ganglion, two nerves are given off: one to the lateral line, the other to the skin over the dorsal part of the branchial chamber at the point where it makes a fold to line the operculum. Two branches are given off from the distal and outer side of the vagal ganglion, which supply the second and third branchial arches; then the greater part of the ganglion tapers off at its distal extremity into the main trunk of the vagus, which after giving a branch to the fourth branchial arch, follows the œsophagus.

It seems quite as reasonable to consider as the glossopharyngeal all the above-mentioned nerves to the branchial arches, which appear to a great extent to be distinct from the main trunk of the vagus; as to confine the interpretation to the branch which supplies the first branchial arch alone, which is usually the custom.

The nerve which is situated behind the vagus is generally looked upon as a spinal nerve, although in many Teleostei, in the present species among the number, it passes out of the skull through a special foramen in the exoccipital bone; here it is clearly a double nerve. It arises by two dorsal and two ventral roots; these all join into one trunk, which has a ganglionic enlargement as it emerges through the foramen. Immediately outside it gives off a dorsal branch like a spinal nerve; after which it divides into two trunks, which run a parallel course dorsad of the kidney, and then unite together and with the main trunk of the succeeding nerve, which is the first nerve that emerges through the vertebral column.   It may be looked upon as the second spinal nerve, or if the first is considered to be two nerves this would be the third. The trunk formed by the union of these nerves constitutes a sort of brachial plexus, and supplies the muscles of the pectoral fin, after having given off a branch which runs down the anterior edge of the shoulder-girdle towards the muscles surrounding the glossohyal bone.

This nerve is certainly a spinal nerve, as far as its origin goes, for it has both dorsal and ventral roots, and in this species it appears to be a combination of two nerves, as is shown by its four roots, and by its trunk dividing into two and joining again.   In some other species—the *Scorpæna Porcus*, for instance—this nerve gives a branch which is distributed quite as far as the anterior part of the glossohyal.

In examining a dissection of the nerves from the upper surface one is struck with the resemblance between the trifacial, the vagus, and the spinal nerves, in respect to their dorsal branches.   Thus we find that in proceeding from behind forward these branches are given off at a gradually decreasing distance from their ganglia ; in the spinal nerves their dorsal branch is given off distad of the ganglion ; in the first spinal nerve and the vagus it comes off from the ganglion itself, and in the trifacial it divides from the main trunk proximad of the ganglion.

In the Whiting (*Merlangus vulgaris*) the arrangement of the three nerves in relation to each other differs more from that of the *M. Pollachius* than would be supposed possible in species of the same genus.   In this species, the so-called facial of Stannius arises in common with the remainder of the trifacial ; being the penultimate root of that nerve, it passes over the casserian ganglion as a distinct cord without in any way communicating with it.   It then emerges through the foramen with the remaining branches of the trifacial ; after that, it receives the branch from the ganglion of the so-called glossopharyngeal, which is well developed in this species ; it then divides into two branches : one pursues its course along the posterior and outer edge of the orbit ; the other, after perforating the palato-quadrate arch, passes down on the outside of that structure to disappear from view outside the quadrate bone.

The acusticus does not send a communicating branch to the vagus, but its posterior cord is closely applied to the anterior root of the latter, until it arrives at the ampulla of the posterior semicircular canal, when it leaves its companion to be distributed on that structure.   The two trunks are very easily separated from each other, and there is no nervous connexion between them.

In this species both roots of the vagus pass through the ear cavity over the otolithic sac : a disposition which is caused by the extreme backward prolongation of the latter. The so-called glossopharyngeal, or branch to the first branchial arch, is given off by the posterior root of the vagus immediately before its junction with the anterior root of that nerve ; it passes forward along the inner surface of the outer wall of the ear cavity, and emerges through the foramen in that wall, outside of which it forms the ganglion, as in *M. Pollachius*.   From this ganglion the nerve for the first branchial arch is given off from its posterior end, while the branch which joins the facial root of the trifacial comes off from its anterior side.

Thus we have here a corresponding nerve given off from two distinct sources in allied species, so that it seems not beyond the bounds of possibility, with such varying elements (evolution being granted), that the branchial divisions of the vagus should be detached from that trunk, and absorbing the branch of the acusticus to the first branchial arch should become developed in the higher Vertebrata as the glosso-pharyngeal; and, on the other hand, that the facial division of the trifacial should become detached from that origin, and attach itself entirely to the anterior cord of the same branch of the acusticus; the two halves of the latter being separated. Then the communicating twig between the glossopharyngeal and the facial remains as evidence of their former union.

Microscopic Anatomy of the Brain.
Lobi Olfactorii.

The lobi olfactorii (fig. 1, *ol.*) consist essentially of three layers. Of these the external is thicker in front, and is formed by the fibres of the olfactory nerve (fig. 1, *n.* 1), which on entering diverge in all directions and form a sort of envelope for the anterior part of the lobe. More internal comes a layer of finely granular neuroglia, which surrounds on the upper, anterior, and lower sides a mass of small cells, which occupy the central and posterior part of the lobe, being separated from the hinder edge by a narrow stratum of fibres, which descend to the postero inferior angle, and pass out to form the commissure between this lobe and the cerebrum (fig. 15, *ab.*).

The cells of the central group are small in size, resembling to a certain extent those of the cerebrum. Many are oval or circular in outline, but generally they are more or less pear-shaped. Each cell has a nucleus of comparatively large size, which is invariably situated at the broader end of the cell; the protoplasm or cell-contents occupy the narrower side, which terminates in a more or less blunt point, from which a single free fibril emerges. The nucleus contains a single spot-like nucleolus, situated near the centre, which occasionally shows symptoms of breaking up into its constituent granules. The total average length of these cells is 0·007 millim. or 0·008 millim., their diameter 0·004 millim. or 0·005 millim.; the nuclei are generally round, or nearly so; and their diameter averages 0·004 millim.

Many of these cells occupy spaces in the neuroglia which probably correspond to the spaces surrounding the cells of the cerebrum described by OBERSTEINER (78) and BEVAN LEWISS (84). Occasionally, nearly the whole of the cell projects into this chamber, but more generally only the broad end, so that the nucleus alone would be bathed in lymph in the latter case. The granules which to a great extent compose the neuroglia of the olfactory lobes become aggregated together, and form a smooth surface on the walls of these spaces; they do not actually form an epithelial layer, but seem to be a rudimentary form of that structure.

A layer of neuroglia surrounds this group of cells, as before mentioned, on all sides except posteriorly, in which with high powers only very fine granules are to be observed. The above described cells occur very sparingly here.

The external portion of the lobule (fig. 1, *o.l.*) is formed principally by the fibres of the olfactory nerve. These fibres enter at the anterior end, and occupy about half the length of the lobe ; they do not go straight, but the bundle dividing at the apex forms an interlacing layer which encloses the fore part of the lobe as in a sheath, and envelopes small rounded masses of coarse granular neuroglia, which may be looked upon as representing the glomeruli in the bulbus olfactorius of Mammalia, described by MEYNERT (81).

Larger cells are seen to occupy the inner edge of this layer of nerve-fibres, where it begins to pass over into the stratum of finely granular neuroglia above described ; at this part the neuroglia is coarser, and the cells in question occupy spaces therein in the same way that the small cells do in the central group. These cells (fig. 15, *e.f.*) are mostly tripolar, with sometimes one, and sometimes two broad protoplasmic processes, the others being fine and probably axis-cylinder prolongations. They measure 0·013 millim. long by 0·010 millim. broad, the nucleus measuring 0·007 millim. by 0·006 millim. ; some have a distinct spot-like nucleolus, which, however, in many specimens cannot be so easily distinguished. Besides these, other unipolar cells (fig. 15, *c.*) occur in which the protoplasm greatly preponderates, and where the nucleus is not much larger than that of the small cells of the central group. The specimen figured has a spot-like nucleolus placed nearly in the centre of the nucleus. In addition to the larger cells, which as before mentioned occupy the border of the layer of fibres, some of these fibres themselves show cell-like swellings (fig. 15, *d.*) in their course, which somewhat resemble the cells described by MEYNERT (81) in the glomeruli olfactorii of the human subject. These cell-like swellings in the course of the fibres are like some kinds of bipolar cells : they have large oval nuclei and conspicuous nucleoli. The length of the one figured is 0·020 millim. and the width 0·006 millim., the nucleus measuring 0·006 millim. by 0·004 millim.

In the Whiting Pollack (*Merlangus Pollachius*) the olfactory lobes are situated beyond the cranial cavity, close over the nasal sacs, and are connected to the cerebral lobes by two long commissures. Here the structure very much resembles that of those lobes in the Grey Mullet (*Mugil cephalus*), above described. In these, also, the group of small cells is found to be surrounded by the layer of finely granular neuroglia ; and outside of all comes the fibres of the olfactory nerve.

That these lobes homologise the bulbi olfactorii of Mammalia will be seen by comparing a section through the olfactory lobe of the Teleostean, with a similar section through the bulbus olfactorius of the monkey, as described by MEYNERT (81). According to that author a section from outside inwards shows first, the olfactory nerve layer ; next, a stratum glomerulosum containing glomeruli olfactorii, then a stratum gelatinosum in which the ganglion cells are more closely aggregated internally, finally a layer of medullary fibres. A section through the olfactory lobe of a Teleostean observed from before backwards, is comparable to the above-described section made from without inwards ; first come the layer of fibres from the olfactory nerve comparable to the external layer, then the layer of nodulated masses of neuroglia and coarse granules comparable to the stratum glomerulosum, then the finely granular neuroglia with sparsely scattered cells, comparable to the external part of the stratum glomerulosum, then the central group of small cells comparable to the internal part of the same stratum, and finally the thin layer of fibres which form the commissure to the cerebral lobes, which are comparable to the internal layer of medullary fibres above mentioned.

Cerebrum or Cerebral Lobes.

The lobi cerebri are invested under the pia mater by a single layer of epithelial cells of the columnar variety ; each of these cells gives off from its inner extremity a long fine process, which passing into the substance of these lobes is lost in the neuroglia. A finely granular neuroglia occupies the greater part of the cerebral lobes, in which cells of various sizes are scattered in varying proportions ; these cells range in size from 0·014 millim. long by 0·010 millim. broad, to 0·007 millim. by 0·005 millim. ; the smallest cells (fig. 16, a.) are generally pyriform in shape, each with a comparatively large nucleus, to one side of which a conical, more or less elongated mass of protoplasm is attached, from the pointed end of which a nerve-fibre emerges.

Occasionally, cells (fig. 16, b.) occur which have two diverging processes, the nucleus being attached to the middle and projecting two-thirds of its circumference from the protoplasm. These smaller cells seldom show a distinct nucleolus, but more often only scattered granules, as if the nucleolus had been broken up. This kind of cell (fig. 17) occurs more frequently near the outer edge of the cerebral lobes, and in some places forms a layer of cells beneath the epithelium three or four deep, with scarcely any neuroglia between them. They do not form a connected layer throughout the border of the cerebral lobes, but only occur in places ; at other parts the neuroglia extends quite to the inner surface of the epithelial cells.

The neuroglia increases in quantity towards the centre of the cerebral lobes, while the cells decrease in number, but at the same time become larger in size ; these are either bipolar or tripolar cells (fig. 16, c.), in which distinct nuclei are visible, which are always placed either on one side of the tripolar or at one end of the bipolar cells. It thus happens that some part of the nucleus always projects, bare of protoplasm, into the space of neuroglia which surrounds the cells on all sides ; generally they are only held in position by their processes, for which the neuroglia often forms hollow sheaths, in which the processes occasionally extend some distance. It seldom happens that a distinct nucleolus is observable in the nucleus, but usually only granules, which sometimes are found grouped together in the centre, as if the nucleolus had just broken up.

That the spaces mentioned above are lymph spaces has been conclusively shown by OBERSTEINER (78), who not only observed lymph corpuscles in the corresponding

ERRATUM.

PHILOSOPHICAL TRANSACTIONS, VOL. 169, 1878.

Page 750, line 5 from top, *for* glomerulosum, *read* gelatinosum.

vacuities of the mammalian cerebrum, but actually injected one of them,—a fact
which demonstrates that STIEDA's idea that they are artificial productions is erro-
neous ; besides, BEVAN LEWISS (84) also shows that they are real structures. The inner
surface of these spaces is rendered smooth by an agglomeration and close apposition of
the granules of the neuroglia, as in the olfactory lobes.

The cells above described occupy a position intermediate between the small cells on
the periphery and the central part of the lobes, which is occupied by white medullary
fibres ; these fibres converge towards the postero-inferior angle, where they form a
medullary cord. They are comparable to the " corona radiata" of the cerebrum ; they
pass downward and backward to be lost in the anterior end of the hypoarium.

The cells become much less numerous in passing towards the centre of these lobes
and are seldom found in the "corona radiata ;" those that do occur, however, have an
elongated shape (fig. 16, d.), both protoplasm and nucleus appearing as if they had
been pressed out by the surrounding fibres. The neuroglia, which occupies a large
part of these lobes, is composed of a granular substance, in which extremely fine fibres
ramify in all directions, forming a network uniting together the smaller cells above
described. The transverse commissure which connects the lobe of one side to that of
the other is formed of two bundles of fibres placed one behind the other ; the anterior
bundle passes on each side forward into the anterior part of each lobe, and is lost in
the walls of the fissure between the two lobes, while the posterior bundle passes more
directly into the central parts.

It will be seen that the structure of these lobes differs considerably from that of the
lobi olfactorii. Here, there are no incipient glomeruli olfactorii, neither are there cell-
like swellings of the nerve-fibres, nor a central group of cells ; but these bodies are
more dispersed, are mostly of a different character, and are collected more towards the
circumference. Thus, histological investigation does not support the opinion of some
of the older anatomists, that these tuberosities homologise the bulbi olfactorii. The
crura of the lobi olfactorii (fig. 1, ce.) pass from the posterior end of those lobes in a
curved manner to the posterior end of the cerebral lobes, crossing over the fibres of the
" corona radiata;" they cross these fibres, but have no direct communication with them,
but continue their course into the posterior lateral lobule of the cerebrum, where they
are lost.

Tectum Lobi Optici.

The structure of the tectum lobi optici differs in different parts of its extent ; taken
at about the centre of its arch, it shows (fig. 18) seven layers, commencing on the
outside.

The first layer consists of finely granular neuroglia placed in immediate contact
with the pia mater covering the tectum.

The second layer consists of coarse fibres apparently transverse but really oblique,
that is, going in a direction between transverse and longitudinal ; this layer contains
sparsely distributed fusiform cells with their long axes placed radially.

The third layer consists of granular matter, with closely packed fibres, arranged radially so as to give it a smoothly striated appearance.

The fourth layer has the radial fibres not very closely placed, and the remainder of the layer consists of obliquely directed fibres, as in the second layer.

The fifth layer consists of transverse fibres derived from the crura lobi optici. This layer is clearer in colour than the remainder of the tectum, owing to the absence of granular matter, and also to the fibres not becoming so readily coloured as the other parts of the tectum ; some radial fibres run across this stratum also.

The sixth layer consists of small cells arranged on branched stems which are prolonged into the radial fibres occurring in the other layers.

The seventh is a layer of connective tissue of varying thickness in different parts of the tectum ; it forms on its external edge a support for the cells of the sixth layer, and internally terminates by a single layer of epithelial cells which form a smooth surface towards the ventricle of the optic lobe ; this " ependyma " forms a support for the radiating fibres of the crura lobi optici in their passage from the torus semicircularis to the tectum ; this connective tissue is composed of an inextricable network of fibrillæ derived from its epithelial layer of cells.

STIEDA (58) makes eight strata in the tectum by the expedient of dividing the ependyma into two, making the epithelial layer of cells distinct from the connective tissue beneath them ; but as the fibrillæ of this layer are derived from the cells, it seems scarcely correct to separate them. In other respects his division corresponds very closely to mine.

The cells of the sixth layer are of two different forms : those situated on the inner edge which make the terminal enlargement of the radial fibres, and those of the deeper part of the stratum which are attached to the sides of the fibres of the first, like grapes to their stalk.

The cells (fig. 18, b.) which make up the inner row of this layer may be described as fusiform, oval, or rhomboidal in shape ; they generally show a distinct oval nucleus in which also a distinct spot-like nucleolus is visible : they vary in length from 0·010 millim. to 0·015 millim., and in width from 0·002 millim. to 0·005 millim. ; the nucleus measures in length from 0·004 millim. to 0·005 millim., and from 0·003 millim. to 0·004 millim. in width ; the connective tissue of the seventh layer is attached to the inner end of some of the cells, while their outer end passes off into a fibre which runs radially towards the external surface of the tectum, and probably extends as far as the second layer.

The fibres of these cells have a tendency to run in bundles formed of several united together ; the bulk of this stratum is made up of cells (fig. 18, c.) of a smaller size than those described, and generally more rounded ; these are attached to the fibres of the former cells sometimes by a short stalk, and in other cases they are sessile ; they usually measure 0·004 millim. by 0·003 millim., with but slight variation in size.

There is present in most cases a distinct nucleus, which is generally rounded, but sometimes it presents a tendency to the oval form ; these nuclei often show a distinct nucleolus. About ten or twelve of these cells occupy the thickness of this sixth layer ; towards the anterior part of the tectum this layer passes continuously into the fornix. (I shall adopt this term in preference to "torus longitudinalis" used by FRITSCH, without attaching any homological meaning to it, but simply as indicating the form of the part to which it is applied ; it has been in use since CARUS first discovered the part, and therefore has the sanction of antiquity in its favour.) The other species (fig. 18, d.) of nervous elements in the tectum is found in the second layer ; these are long, fusiform, cell-like swellings of the radial fibres, which are finer at the inner end than at the outer ; it is somewhat difficult to measure their length owing to the gradual transition between the fibre and the cells, it may however be said to vary between 0·018 millim. and 0·040 millim. ; the width is more constant, being seldom more than 0·005 millim., but occasionally reaching as much as 0·007 millim. ; the nucleus measured about 0·005 millim. by 0·003 millim. These cells are not enclosed in a space, but the neuroglia is in apposition to their external surface. The fibre which passes from the inner end of these cells is the finer, and can be traced into the smoothly striated third layer ; the fibres from the sixth layer can be traced into the same stratum on the other side ; from which circumstance the presumption arises that the small cells of the internal layer stand in connexion with the fusiform bodies just described. STIEDA (58) places these cells in his third or striated layer, and considers that they belong to the neuroglia "grundsubstanz." This does not appear to be quite correct ; they are situated, in fact, in the layer which he terms "die äussere Langsfaserschicht." Their nervous character can scarcely be doubtful ; they resemble in fundamental structure the cell-like swellings on the fibres of the olfactory lobe, and also the Purkinje cells of the second layer of the cerebellum, as the latter would appear if drawn out and stretched so as to be made long and thin. The outer process of these cells can be traced under favourable circumstances into the outer finely-granular layer of the tectum.

The modifications undergone by these layers in various parts of the tectum are as follows :—

At the outer side of the entrance of the crura lobi optici the fifth layer disappears as a distinct stratum, being only formed by the fibres of that part running in an inward direction towards the central commissure of the tectum. Anteriorly towards the inner end the first layer disappears. On the outer side all the layers, except the first, third, and sixth, are obliterated by the fibres of the optic tract. Further back, at about the middle of the tectum, longitudinal fibres appear which are intercalated between the first and second layers ; others occur between the fourth and fifth layers towards the inner edge ; these latter gradually die out and extend only about one-third of the width of the tectum.

The cells of the sixth layer are continuous internally with those of the fornix at the anterior termination of the tectum. The fornix consists of two longitudinal ridges of a somewhat triangular shape projecting into the ventricle of the optic lobe, and are placed along the inner and contiguous margins of the two halves of the tectum. The border of each ridge, which is turned towards the ventricle, is lined by a delicate layer of columnar epithelial cells, which lie immediately upon the nervous elements, without the intervention of any connective tissue.

The cells (fig. 19) which constitute the fornix are mostly of a spherical form, consisting almost entirely of nuclei with only a narrow rim of protoplasm round them ; they generally contain a spot-like nucleolus ; they usually measure 0·003 millim. or 0·004 millim. in diameter. Occasionally larger cells occur, which present a triangular shape from the greater quantity of protoplasm belonging to them. One of these is seen in the figure. These cells are arranged in rows, or in single files radiating from the upper and inner angle of the fornix ; each row is separated from its neighbour by bundles of fibrillæ, which also radiate from the same point ; these bundles are thicker at the proximal end, and gradually become smaller by giving off radiating fibrils in their course. The cells are attached to these fibrils sometimes by short branchlets, and sometimes they are sessile. The fornix forms a link connecting the sixth layer of the tectum to the granular layer of the valvula cerebelli, by which they are further continuous with the third layer in the cerebellum.

Tori Semicirculares.

The tori semicirculares (fig. 20, a.) may be considered as the anterior termination of the medulla oblongata ; they are tuberosities of a more or less semicircular shape, which project into the floor of the ventricle of the optic lobe ; they are principally composed of grey matter, through which the bundles of the crura lobi optici pass on their way to the internal surface of the tectum lobi optici. The surface turned towards the ventricle is lined by a stratum of connective tissue (fig. 20, ep.), which is continuous with the corresponding lining of the tectum ; its margin is bordered by a layer of columnar epithelial cells, the internally directed extremities of which pass into and form the fibrillæ of the connective tissue, as in the seventh layer of the tectum. This appears to correspond to the "ependyma ventriculorum." The principal characteristics of the tori semicirculares are small cells (fig. 20, b.), elongated, narrow, and tapering at their pointed extremities into long fibres, which can be traced through the substance of the torus to the level of the bundles of nerve-fibres which belong to the crura lobi optici ; they have a circular or oval nucleus which usually occupies the whole width of the thickest part of the cell ; the nucleolus is generally represented by a few granules. They vary in length from 0·009 millim. to 0·016 millim., and in width from 0·004 millim. to 0·006 millim. ; they are arranged in a row along the margin of the torus, and in the interior there are two or three, more or less complete, nearly horizontal rows of the same species of cells. The deeper part of this tuberosity is occupied by bundles of nerve-fibres belonging to the crura lobi optici, which pass through them on their way to the internal surface of the tectum.   Between them, and beneath the more superficial bundles, are scattered cells which resemble the larger cells in the cerebrum in size and shape.

In the Basse (*Labrax Lupus*) the smaller cells on the surface are not placed in a row, but in groups, leaving spaces between them bare of cells, or in which only a few isolated ones occur; they are also found in groups in the interior, but not in connected rows.   As if to make up for this deficiency a few large cells are found in the interior, which slightly exceed in size the larger ones in the cerebrum ; they are pyriform in shape, and have a nucleus and a distinct nucleolus, resembling, on a smaller scale, the cells in the spinal cord.   In a section taken through the whole length of the torus about six of these cells were found in one plane.   The parenchyma of the tori semicirculares is composed of coarse granular neuroglia, in which fibres, mostly longitudinal, are indistinctly visible, chiefly towards the more superficial part.   As in *Mugil*, the deeper part of the torus is occupied by the bundles of fibres of the crura lobi optici. Beneath the more superficial bundles of these, there occurs a thin layer of grey substance in which other cells are found, which are slightly larger than those just mentioned; they have a nucleus, nucleolus, and two or three processes; each cell occupies a space in the neuroglia ; they are much less numerous than in the *Mugil*, and occur in groups of two or three.   Two groups and a single cell occur in a longitudinal section through the whole torus in one plane.

The Hypoaria.

The parenchyma of the hypoaria is composed of finely granular neuroglia, in which the ramifications of extremely small fibres form a network of inextricable tenuity.   In this neuroglia bundles of nerve-fibres radiate from the posterior and upper side in distinct and well-formed cords.   The nerve cells (fig. 21, *a*.) occur throughout the neuroglia scattered singly, but increasing in number towards the free margin of the hypoarium.   These cells are pyriform in shape ; the thicker end is occupied by a nucleus, in the centre of which, in most cases, a spot-like nucleolus is seen ; occasionally, however, this is represented by a group of granules.   Each cell partly occupies a distinct chamber in the neuroglia, into which only the nucleus projects, the pointed end being closely surrounded by neuroglia ; occasionally a process, given off from the thicker end, converts them into bipolar cells.   Their average length is 0·008 millim., and their width 0·005 millim. ; the nucleus usually has a diameter of 0·004 millim.

The external surface of the hypoaria is not covered by an epithelial layer.   Each lobe presents a ventricle which commences close to the inferior surface, where it extends from near the anterior to near the posterior end ; behind, this ventricle is narrow and slightly curved inwards ; anteriorly, it expands and becomes broader ; each ventricle gives off a passage from its anterior end, which passes with a curve upwards and inwards until the passage of one side meets that of the other in the infundibulum.

These ventricles are lined by a distinct layer of epithelium, which is a continuation of the epithelium lining the central canal of the spinal cord.   They are surrounded by a layer of small circular or pear-shaped cells (fig. 21, *b.*), which extend for some distance into the substance of the hypoaria; these cells abound more especially along the ventricles themselves, close to the lower surface of these tuberosities, but they also occur in the course of the passages which communicate with the infundibulum.   They measure about 0·006 millim. in length and 0·005 millim. in width, and have comparatively large nuclei of about 0·004 millim. in diameter.   Some have a spot-like nucleolus, which in other specimens is represented only by a group of granules.   Cells (fig. 21 *c.*) somewhat resembling those of the terminal row of the sixth layer of the tectum occur beneath the epithelial lining of the infundibulum and the ante-chamber, or ventricle as it may be called, of the hypophysis cerebri; they are bipolar, tripolar, or quadripolar; but one process, that directed away from the infundibulum, can be traced much further than the others; they vary from 0·008 millim. to 0·022 millim. in length, and from 0·006 millim. to 0·009 millim. in width; they have distinct, well-marked nuclei, the diameter of the larger being 0·006 millim., that of the smaller specimens being 0·004 millim.; in most cases the nucleolus is represented by a few granules, either scattered through the nucleus or collected into a group.

In addition to these small cells, others of a much larger size (fig. 21, *d.*) occur, which are situated more particularly under the epithelium of the ventricle of the hypophysis cerebri, and the adjacent anterior edge of the hypoarium; some are pear-shaped, others are expanded at one end and flattened like an enlarged columnar epithelial cell, but they are not of the nature of epithelium, for they lie beneath that layer.   The largest measure 0·030 millim. in length, by 0·014 millim. in width; the nucleus is large, and the nucleolus also is disk-like and measures 0·002 millim. in diameter.

Each hypoarium contains a peculiar spherical body (fig. 22), denominated by FRITSCH "nucleus rotundus."   This is placed nearer the posterior edge and the mid-line than the external surface and the anterior end; it is composed of interlacing fibres and granules, in which are embedded cell-like bodies which differ very greatly in size, some measuring as much as 0·07 millim. by 0·06 millim., some as little as 0·04 millim. by 0·03 millim.; many are nearly round, others longer than broad; they are composed of loosely aggregated granules of about 0·001 millim. or 0·002 millim. in diameter, which are crowded round the circumference, leaving a space in the centre, which in many cases is occupied by a smooth oval or pyriform body, having somewhat the aspect of the protoplasm of a cell, but in which no nucleus is observable; sometimes this body is missing in very thin sections, there remaining only a clear space, which it had probably occupied.   Capillaries are occasionally to be seen passing through the loose granules of the circumferential portion.

What these bodies are I am at a loss to determine; they are of about the same size as the larger cells of the spinal cord.   The granules also which compose their cortex resemble those of the protoplasm of those cells, in size and aspect, except that they are more loosely aggregated: they might be looked upon as cells in which the granules of the protoplasm are more loosely arranged than in an ordinary cell ; or the body in the centre might be regarded as a cell, surrounded by a mass of granules for reinforcing or extending its nervous energy.

In *Mugil cephalus* these bodies occupy the whole of the " nucleus rotundus," but in *Crenilabrus* there is a space left in the centre occupied only by granules and a network of fibres.

In *Crenilabrus* the circumference of this body is bounded by a layer of small cells (fig. 22, *c.*), varying in length from 0·010 millim. to 0·016 millim., and in width from 0·004 millim. to 0·005 millim. ; they are elongated in shape, and have a circular nucleus, which contains several granules instead of a single nucleolus. This nucleus often projects from one end of the cell, giving to the latter a high-shouldered appearance ; the side of the cell opposite its nucleus ends in one or two processes, and is always turned towards the centre of the " nucleus rotundus." These cells absorb colouring matter to a greater extent than most others. In *Mugil* they exist, but do not form a connected layer round the body in question, as is the case in *Crenilabrus.*

Cerebellum.

The cerebellum presents a structure comparable to that found in Mammalia. In a section (fig. 23) through this tuberosity, four layers are observable from the external surface to the centre.

The first layer (fig. 23, *a.*) consists of straight fibres, arranged perpendicularly to the long axis of this division of the brain ; these fibres are embedded in a coarse granular neuroglia.

The second layer (fig. 23, *b.*) is composed of large bipolar cells of peculiar structure, corresponding to the cells of Purkinje in the cerebellum of Mammalia. These form a stratum three or four cells in thickness throughout the cerebellum, except at the superior and inferior angles, where they are accumulated to a greater extent.

The third layer (fig. 23, *c.*) is constituted by a mass of minute cells, and ramifications of fine fibrillæ.

The fourth layer is formed by a bundle of fibres which go into the anterior crus cerebelli.

The bipolar cells have the usual structure of those of Purkinje (fig. 23, *d.*) in the mammalian cerebellum. They are elongated bodies, containing a large nucleus, in which a well-developed nucleolus is observable ; one end tapers into a fine process, while the other passes off more gradually to a thick one. This latter, after passing some distance in the same layer, either towards the anterior or posterior end, parallel to the long axis of the cerebellum, enters the external layer, and, dividing dichotomously, becomes finer and still more fine, as it continues at right angles to the surface, and passes towards the outer edge, where it eventually disappears from view. At the point of bifurcation of these fibres a swelling occurs which fills up the angle formed by the divergence of the two branches; at the external edge the fibres are sometimes seen to form loops turning back towards the centre.

The Purkinje cells in Teleostei differ from those in the cerebellum of Mammalia in being less complicated, inasmuch as their thick processes do not divide into two branches, giving off a forest of straight fibres, but continue as a single trunk for some distance, and enter the external layer before dividing, and that only dichotomously. Moreover, they are placed with their long axis parallel to the long axis of the cerebellum, instead of transversely to that axis, as in Mammalia. They resemble, in fact, the cells of the corresponding layer in the cerebellum of the newly-born infant in the simplicity of the arrangement of their prolongations.

The third layer (fig. 23, e.) is composed of cells of extreme minuteness, which possess a nucleus, a nucleolus, and a small quantity of protoplasm. They are usually pear-shaped, and from the pointed end an extremely fine fibre proceeds; which fibre, with those of the other cells in this layer, join together in a network which forms ramifications in the neuroglia of this stratum. Occasionally some of these cells are seen to be attached by their points to the side of a fibrilla.

The theory I adopt as to the arrangement of the elements of the cerebellum is this: The broad processes of the cells of Purkinje divide continuously until they arrive near to the external edge, by which time they have become extremely fine; they then turn back, and form a network in this layer, and, passing between the cells of Purkinje, finally join the corpuscles of the third layer, uniting them together in an inextricable network.

The above theory is based on the following circumstances. In teased-out preparations, the broad fibres of the Purkinje cells are found to be covered by coarse granules, which are attached to them at a certain distance from the cell, at points nearer to which they are smooth. These granules resemble those found in the neuroglia of the external layer. The cells of the third layer are seen, when teased out, to be united together by fine fibres, which are quite smooth, having no attached granules. Thus it is found that the characteristic elements of the external layer are fibres to which coarse granules are attached, giving them a granulated appearance; while the third layer is distinguished by cells the fibrils of which are smooth.

In some preparations of teased-out Purkinje cells the broad fibre is seen to become more and more decreased in size, and the finest fibres have granules attached. On the other hand, preparations of the cells of the third layer have been made in which fibrils longer than usual have been preserved unbroken; these, smooth near their origin, have become covered with granules, resembling those of the first layer, at a greater or less distance from the cell. From this it may be inferred that the latter fibres pass from the third layer into the first. But on the above supposition, what becomes of the fine fibres of the Purkinje cells? GERLACH (71) made out that they joined the cells and network of the third layer, which if the above description be anywhere near the truth cannot be the case, and his opinion is not confirmed by DEITERS (73).

The latter author and KOSCHENIKOFF (75) demonstrated that they join double contoured nerve-fibres,—a fact which would accord well with the above-mentioned views, and would imply that they join, not the small cells of the third, but the fibres of the fourth layer, and thus a junction would be formed in a roundabout manner between the minute elements of the third layer and the commissures of the other parts of the brain. According to HADLICH (77) the arrangement is similar to that above given, but he does not explain what becomes of the finer fibres of the Purkinje cells. OBERSTEINER (78) describes small cells or corpuscles in the outer or first layer in the cerebellum of the fœtus, to which the fibres from the broad processes of the Purkinje cells are attached,—a fact which SANKEY (83) has confirmed in the adult. I have not found any cells of this description in the external layer of the cerebellum in Teleostei ; but their presence would not interfere with the interpretation adopted here, for the fibres in question could yet pass through those corpuscles, and behave as above mentioned.

The whole cerebellum in the Teleostei appears to correspond to a single lobulus in that division of the brain in the human subject.

In *Mugil cephalus* there are indications of the commencement of a second lobulus, which in *Labrax Lupus* are more decided.

There is a vertical fissure in the central line of the cerebellum in *Mugil*, forming a ventricle, which extends from the posterior end as far forward as the posterior edge of the crura cerebelli ; it has an appearance as if the two halves had not properly united.

The Valvula Cerebelli.

The valvula cerebelli has precisely the same structure that the cerebellum itself has ; the layer of straight fibres, the layer of Purkinje cells, and the layer of minute cells are all present : the only difference to be seen lies in the arrangement of these strata.

The layer of straight fibres is a direct continuation of the external layer of the cerebellum, which, passing forward into the ventricle of the optic lobe nearly as far as its anterior extremity, turns back on itself and forms a fold ; so that the edges which would be external in the cerebellum face each other, leaving a narrow fissure between them which communicates with the external surface between the posterior end of the tectum, and the anterior surface of the cerebellum, by a foramen which is closed in by pia mater and gives access to vessels. The Purkinje cells bear the same relation to the layers of straight fibres that they do to the external layer of the cerebellum. Then the mass of small cells resembling those found in the third layer come to be placed on the surface facing the ventricle of the optic lobe, and extend as wings on each side. In the *Mugil* these wings are simple rounded bodies, but in the *Labrax* a deep transverse fold of straight fibres divides them into two lobes, and in the *Crenilabrus* two such folds divide them into three lobes. This also appears to be the case in the Carp. They are the bodies termed by HALLER "cornu ammonis," and I have reason to suppose that they form the peculiar organ found in the brain of the *Mormyridæ*, as I have before mentioned.

Tuberosities of the Vagus and the Medulla Oblongata.

The tuberosities of the vagus (fig. 10, *t.v.*) resemble very much the tori semi-circulares in structure. The sides forming the walls of the fissure constituting the posterior part of the fourth ventricle are lined by a layer of connective tissue bounded internally by a single row of epithelial cells, precisely in the same way that the surface of the torus facing the ventricle of the optic lobe is covered. A vertical row of cells is placed externally to this ependyma of the same kind as those found beneath that structure in the torus. The only difference that exists between these two tuberosities is, that in the one belonging to the vagus the groups of cells project more beyond the level of the nervous tissue into the ependyma than in the torus, and also that the larger cells which exist in the latter are not found in the former. That part of the medulla oblongata which bridges over the narrow part of the fourth ventricle consists entirely of granular matter, and no cells of any kind are to be seen in it.

Transverse Commissures of the Central Nervous System.

In the anterior part of the spinal cord only two commissures are visible—one about half way between the central canal and the ventral edge of the cord; this is the ventral commissure (fig. 1, *v.t.c.*) which connects the ventral horns of grey matter of the two sides. The other is visible only in sections which pass through the dorsal roots of the nerves, and connects the dorsal horns of grey matter of the two sides. This latter commissure is more pronounced nearer the fourth ventricle, and immediately behind the fissure of the medulla oblongata it comes to be closely applied to the dorsal edge of the central canal.

The two commissures mentioned by MAUTHNER (50) are not visible in *Mugil*; the place which he indicates for them being occupied in this species by connective tissue : the "substantia gelatinosa centralis" of STILLING. This connective tissue is composed of fibres derived from the epithelial layer surrounding the central canal of the cord.

Immediately behind the posterior fissure of the fourth ventricle a series of transverse commissures come to view, which gradually take the place of the ventral commissures of the cord, although they do not occupy exactly the same relative position. They connect the tuberosities of the vagi together and increase in size, pari passu, with the latter; they pass downward and across to the other side ventrad of the central longitudinal column.

At about the middle of the vagus territory they unite the root of one nerve to that of the other. At this point one of the branches of the above-mentioned commissures turns back at the dorso-exterior angle of the tuberosity of the vagus, passes downward along the external edge of the medulla to its ventral edge, whence it passes over to the corresponding point on the opposite side. The first-mentioned transverse commissures extend at intervals as far forward as the posterior end of the ganglion of the motores oculorum ; the most anterior bundles become smaller, and pass above instead of beneath the central longitudinal column. Those situated in the region of the crura cerebelli could not be traced directly into them.

Commissura Ansulata. (Figs. 1, 2, and 5, *c.a.*)

There is a double system of transverse commissures at the region of the origin of the motores oculorum and the posterior end of the tectum which are derived from the anterior part of the latter body. They are the commissura ansulata of GOTTSCH (34). Commencing the description of the outer circle of these commissures from the system of transverse fibres passing across the base of the fornix, we can trace the fibres through the fifth layer of the tectum, then by numerous bundles into the torus, where they form the system of the crura lobi optici, then downwards and backwards along the external edge of the medulla to its ventral surface, on the roof of the furrow between the medulla and the hypoarium, where after giving a few fibres to the motor oculi of the opposite side, they cross over to return to the region whence they started. The other part of this double commissure follows the same course as the last, until it attains the lower part of the external edge of the medulla, and there it turns inwards towards the mid-line ; it then crosses obliquely to the other side, and attains the inner part of the torus, near the point of junction of the alæ of the valvula cerebelli with that body, and extends nearly as far forward as the anterior end of the optic lobe. The latter commissure extends in the medulla to about one quarter the length of the space occupied by the former ; they are derived from bundles of longitudinal fibres which first appear on the lateral borders of the medulla oblongata opposite the narrow part of the forth ventricle (fig. 9, *c.a.*).

Some writers compare this commissure to the pons varolii ; this can scarcely be a true homology, since none of the fibres come from the cerebellum. It seems to me more probable that they homologise the decussation of the anterior pyramids ; they resemble to a slight extent the figures of that decussation given by LOCKHART CLARKE (70). BAUDELOT (61) was also of this opinion ; he termed them " commissure antérieure des pyramides;" he appears only to have been acquainted with the first described one. The objection that occurs to me is that they are too far forward in front of, instead of behind the fourth ventricle ; they also come from the optic lobes.

At the anterior end of the floor of the optic lobes are two transverse commissures, one superficial and one deep. The superficial commissure (fig. 3, *p.c.*) passes over the posterior part of the third ventricle, and the passage that puts it into communication with the ventricle of the optic lobe. This passage is, in fact, the anterior end of the

5 E 2

aqueduct of Sylvius. The commissure in question is derived from two separate regions. The anterior part connects the two sides of the anterior end of the floor of the ventricle of the optic lobe (*Thalamus opticus, Stieda*). The posterior part connects the anterior termination of the central longitudinal columns of the cord, or at least of some few fibres which are the continuation forward of those columns. The deeper commissure (figs. 3 and 24, *c.pr.*) is derived from the region about the anterior part of the floor of the optic lobe ; it then passes downwards and backwards, and passing through the " nucleus rotundus " of the hypoarium, turns downwards and forwards, and crosses over in front of the infundibulum to the corresponding point on the opposite side.

CUVIER (28), GOTTSCHE (34), and other anatomists considered that the former homologised the anterior commissure of the cerebrum, but it appears to me that its position corresponds better with the posterior commissure ; its situation at the posterior end of the third ventricle, and behind the infundibulum, points in that direction ; and if, as STIEDA maintains, the region round this ventricle comprising the anterior part of the floor of the optic ventricle homologises the thalami optici, this interpretation would be strengthened, for the commissure in question connects the two sides of that region.

Longitudinal Columns and their Anterior Prolongations.

The anterior columns of the cord are composed of two bundles of large fibres (fig. 1, &c.), one of which is situated close to the ventral edge, the other is situated internally beneath the substantia gelatinosa centralis ; they are separated from each other by the ventral commissures ; the former may be called the ventral longitudinal columns, and the latter the central longitudinal columns. In the latter are situated the giant fibres, two in number, one in each column. These were first described by MAUTHNER (50) ; they are oval in section, measuring 0·016 millim. by 0·012 millim. ; each is contained in a separate tube of connective tissue, which is much larger and more regular in outline than the tubes surrounding the remaining fibres of these bundles ; the other nerve-fibres in these columns vary in size from 0·010 millim. by 0·005 millim. to 0·003 millim. in diameter : thus there is a gradation in size from the small nerves to those nearly as large as the Mauthner fibres. The smaller ones are more numerous in the lateral part of the ventral columns. The Mauthner fibres do not seem to correspond, as MAUTHNER thought, to the large fibres in the spinal cord of the myxinoid fishes, which are described by MÜLLER (36) as flat band-like fibres, which these are not.

The Mauthner fibres (fig. 8) decussate at about opposite the posterior end of the origin of the trifacial, after which they disappear entirely, and I could trace them no farther ; probably they break up into fine fibrillæ of which they are most likely composed. In support of this opinion I may cite a case in which I saw one of these fibres in the spinal cord of *Scorpæna* distinctly break up into fibrillæ for a short distance, and then resume its original appearance.

The ventral longitudinal column rises up gradually from contact with the lower surface of the medulla (fig. 1), and the central longitundal column joins it beneath the posterior part of the cerebellum, beyond the decussation of the Mauthner's fibres; which decussation is not participated in by the accompanying bundles.

The combined columns pass straight forward and are lost in the internal part of the floor of the optic lobe at about the posterior end of the third ventricle.

The columns situated on each side of the central portion of the substantia gelantinosa centralis, which may be termed the lateral columns (fig. 12, *l.c.*), pass forward and are lost in the floor of the optic ventricle near to but outside the last-mentioned columns. At the point where the ventral longitudinal bundles rise up towards the dorsal surface, other fibres are substituted for them along the ventral and lateral borders of the medulla. The more lateral of these, as before mentioned, pass into the commissura ansulata; those in the mid-line, however, pass into the posterior end of the hypoarium through the commissura ansulata, and curve over the anterior end of the furrow between that body and the medulla.

Anterior Crura Cerebelli. (Fig. 24.)

There are three bundles of fibres which may be collectively termed the anterior crura cerebelli, since they pass out of the cerebellum and then turn forward.

The most anterior extending downwards and forwards beneath the anterior layer of the Purkinje cells of the cerebellum, immediately turns forwards and is lost in the lateral wings of the valvula cerebelli.

The most posterior of the three bundles passes obliquely downwards and forwards towards the hypoarium and is lost near the outer side of the "nucleus rotundus" of that lobe.

The middle cord of the anterior crura cerebelli is the largest of the three; it separates into two divisions at the base of that section of the brain. The superior division enters the lateral wing of the valvula cerebelli beneath the anterior bundle of the crus.

The other division, which is the main body of this bundle, enters the deeper parts of the torus, and then making a gentle curve with the concavity turned upwards, it enters the fourth layer of the tectum; this may be looked upon as the processus e cerebello ad testes.

Many bundles of fibres are derived from the deep commissure which was described with the transverse commissures of the brain; of these one passes off when it arrives at the superior edge of the "nucleus rotundus." This bundle on leaving the abovementioned commissure borders the posterior margin of that body, and is joined at the lower edge by several small bundles of fibres, which leave the deep commissure in the "nucleus rotundus," also by bundles of fibres which are derived from the region slightly in advance of the origin of that commissure; these latter cords pass down in front of the "nucleus rotundus," close to its anterior edge, forming a border thereto. The whole of these fibres stream out from the lower edge of the "nucleus rotundus," and disappear in the posterior part of the hypoarium.

Deep origins of the Cerebral Nerves.

The origin of the olfactory nerve (fig. 1, *n*. 1) has been described in the account of the histology of the lobi olfactorii.

The optic nerves (figs. 3 and 4, *n*. 2) are derived from three sources. A few of the inferior fibres come up from the anterior end of the hypoarium. The superior fibres are derived from the three outer layers of the tectum lobi optii; in some sections the fibres for this nerve form an additional distinct stratum of longitudinal fibres intercalated between the first and second layer; this shows more particularly towards the middle of each tectum.

The third root is formed by fibres, which arise in the interior of the torus semicircularis, take a direction outwards towards its external edge, and form a bundle which passes through the crura cerebri, and being intercalated between them and the outer margin of the torus, descend towards the anterior inferior end of the tectum, where it joins the optic tract.

The motores oculorum (figs. 1, 2, and 5, *n*. 3) are derived from a group of medium-sized cells, situated beneath the floor of the aquæductus Sylvii immediately behind its entrance into the ventricle of the optic lobe; from these cells the fibres pass down close to the mid-line towards the ventral surface of the medulla, where they pass through the commissura ansulata; they then emerge from the angle between the medulla and the hypoarium, having received some fibres from the opposite side of the commissure. This nerve has two separate origins: the main origin from the ganglion on its own side, above described, and a smaller one from the region of the crura lobi optici of the opposite side.

The trochleares (fig. 6, *n*. 4) arise from the anterior end of the cerebellum on a level with the base of the valvula cerebelli, where each nerve decussates with its fellow of the opposite side, and becomes intermingled with the transverse commissure of the cerebellum above the aqueduct; the nerve then passes down the margin of the medulla, outside the crura cerebelli, and emerges behind the posterior end of the optic lobe.

The trifacial (figs. 2, 7, 8, and 9, *n*. 5) has three distinct points of origin, of which two belong to the anterior part of its root, and one to the posterior part. The anterior root is made up of two distinct species of fibres; the ventral part of the root is composed of fine slender, while the dorsal half has large, coarse, double contoured fibres. The regions of origin whence these are derived are placed at some distance apart; the latter come in a nearly straight line from a large ganglion situated beneath the floor of the widest part of the fourth ventricle. The cells forming this ganglion are of large size, like those found in the cord. This ganglion bears about the same relation to the floor of the anterior part of the fourth ventricle that the larger cells of the ganglion of origin of the vagus do to the floor of the posterior part of the same ventricle, being, if anything, a little nearer the floor and farther from the mid-line. The fine fibres which form the ventral side of this root are derived from a bundle, which comes forward from the external part of the lateral columns of the spinal cord, and crosses the posterior root of the vagus close to its emergence from the medulla oblongata; it passes ventrad of the anterior root of the latter, then between the origin of the acusticus and the posterior part of the root of this nerve, and then joins the ventral part of the root under discussion. This bundle is very distinct and well-formed between the vagus and the point where it emerges from the medulla, but behind the former it gradually disappears, and is probably derived from the ventral horn of grey matter in the cord. In passing over the vagus it presents a delusive appearance of joining that nerve, all the fibres turning towards the external edge at that point ; but a careful inspection of a series of horizontal sections proves that such is not the case, but that the fibres pass on backwards as described. The posterior root of the trifacial arises as a bundle of fibres, which come forward from the central portion of the vagal tuberosity, and are collected into a cord which passes forward along the side of the narrow part of the fourth ventricle, until it arrives at a point close behind the expanded portion of the same, and opposite the decussation of the fibres of Mauthner, where it turns outward and slightly downward to form part of the posterior roots of the trifacial.

The abducens (figs. 8 and 9, n. 6) arises by two small roots from two little ganglia placed in the ventral grey matter of the medulla oblongata, beneath the narrow part of the fourth ventricle. A small nervous cord emerges from each of these ganglia, and the two unite together to form the trunk of the nerve at its exit from the ventral side of the medulla.

The acusticus (fig. 9, n. 8) is derived from the lateral part of the medulla oblongata in the region of the anterior end of the ganglion from which the posterior root of the vagus arises. Fibres from this source pass upwards and inwards, and forming a distinct bundle become applied to the upper and outer side of the central longitudinal column in the medulla oblongata. This bundle follows that column, keeping entirely distinct therefrom, as far forward as the posterior end of the anterior part of the fourth ventricle ; here it turns outwards and downwards with a curve, and emerges from the medulla as a nerve trunk placed at a lower level than the last-described root of the trifacial.

The vagus (figs. 2, 9, 10, and 11, n. 10) arises by two roots. The anterior is derived from two distinct sources—viz., from the cerebellum, and from the grey matter covering the narrow part of the fourth ventricle. The former appears as two bundles of nerve-fibres which pass back from that part of the cerebellum immediately covering the anterior chamber of the fourth ventricle; the latter comes from the region of grey matter which covers over the narrow passage of that ventricle, and partly from the transverse commissure at that part. The so-called glossopharyngeal also comes out from beneath this root, and is principally derived from the same part and from the lower portion of the same transverse commissure.

The posterior root of the vagus is also derived from two distinct sources. One is a conspicuous ganglion which extends beneath the whole length of the floor of the posterior part of the fourth ventricle, and reaches even for a short distance behind it. This ganglion is narrower transversely than from above downwards; it is composed of cells of a pyriform shape, the points of which run out into fibres which are partly directed outwards and partly outwards and downwards. The fibres from the cells situated on the dorsal part of the ganglion join the nerve more directly than those which are derived from cells situated nearer the ventral side. The vagus receives eight or ten bundles of fibres from this ganglion.

The other source of origin for this root of the vagus is the vertical row of small cells which occurs in the walls of the posterior end of the fourth ventricle or the vagal tuberosity. From these cells bundles of fine fibres pass across to the outer edge of the medulla; just as in the torus the fibres from the corresponding cells pass through to the deep surface of that part. These fibres all join this posterior root of the vagus, which also derives some reinforcement from the transverse commissure of the medulla at this point. If the idea of OWSJANNIKOW (46) be correct, that the sensory roots of the nerves are derived from small cells, while the motor roots come from the larger cells—an idea which receives countenance here from the origins of all the nerves except that of the trochleares—then these are the origins of the sensory fibres of the vagus, while the bundles from the larger-celled ganglion would be motor roots.

LOCKHART CLARKE (60) thinks that this ganglion of the vagus properly belongs to the hypoglossal, because, he says "that the ganglion in question bears the same relation to the floor of the fourth ventricle that the hypoglossal ganglion bears to the central canal;" he also remarks that a branch of the vagus supplies the tongue in fishes. With regard to the first statement I would point out that the ganglion in question is not the only one which bears that relation to the floor of the fourth ventricle or to the central canal; and that from the extent of the territory supplied by the vagus it is scarcely probable that its greatest and most important source of origin would be devoted to such a comparatively unimportant part (in the fish) as the tongue. With regard to the second point, I have never myself found a branch of the vagus going to the tongue, neither have I met such a statement in the writings of any author that I have consulted. The terminal twigs of the nerves that supply the branchial arches are not in point here, as they would belong to the glossopharyngeal nerve and not to the hypoglossal.

The spinal nerves (figs. 12 and 13), including the first spinal, or as some authors call it, the hypoglossal, have all dorsal and ventral roots. The ventral root arises by three bundles, one of which comes from the ventral transverse commissure, the other two come from the ventral horn of grey matter. I could not find a distinct connexion between these roots and the cells existing in the grey matter. In *Mugil* there are generally nine of these cells to be seen in one section, when any were to be seen at all. The *Scorpæna Porcus*, although a sluggish fish, has more cells in the ventral horn of grey matter than the *Mugil*, which is more active.

The dorsal roots of the spinal nerves arise by three or more bundles, which emerge from the outer and dorsal side of the dorsal horn of grey matter. Some of these fibres came from the dorsal commissures, others from the grey matter itself.

No cells are to be seen in this horn in the *Mugil*, but in *Scorpæna Porcus* the unusual circumstance occurs that its spinal cord, at some distance behind the medulla oblongata, presents at its dorsal part, and close to the mid-line, a pair of ganglia, one on each side. These ganglia are formed of large cells, which resemble those only found on the ventral side of the cord in other fishes; they have a distinct nucleus and nucleolus.

Conclusion.

With regard to the homologies of the brain of Teleostei, I have come to very nearly the same conclusion as STIEDA, although my opinion being based solely on researches into the Teleostean nervous system may require some modifications hereafter when I have an opportunity of investigating the brain of Elasmobranchii and Ganoids. The posterior unpaired tuberosity of Teleostei I consider to correspond to the cerebellum, in the ordinary acceptation of the term. The optic lobes would be the corpora quadrigemina, or rather bigemina, and would homologise with the anterior pair. FRITSCH—whose work 'On the Minute Structure of the Brain in Fishes,' only recently published, I have received since the foregoing pages were written, and to which unfortunately I have not yet had time to devote the amount of study which its importance demands—has opposed to this interpretation the consideration that their structure is too complicated; but I think that, if the other conditions of the homologies are satisfied, structure alone would not form a sufficient objection. The other conditions are satisfied : their position at the anterior end of the aqueduct of Sylvius, behind the third ventricle and in front of the cerebellum, points in that direction. The fact that they are comparatively highly organised simply shows that in fishes they perform functions which in higher animals are relegated to other organs. This being the case, the ventricle of these lobes would be simply an extremely enlarged aqueduct of Sylvius, and would correspond to the ventricle of the corpora quadrigemina in the fœtus. The third ventricle is the fissure between the crura cerebri, and would extend between the cerebral lobes as far as the commissure which connects them, which would then homologise the anterior commissure, while the transverse bundle of fibres on the floor of the ventricle of the optic lobe has the relative position of the posterior commissure. FRITSCH has marked the last-named cavity the lateral ventricle, but this appears to be quite untenable; not only its position behind the third ventricle, and the pineal gland, and at the mouth of the aqueduct, is against it, but V. BAER had seen the ventricle in question in the cerebral lobes of the embryonic Teleostean, and WILDER (65) has pointed them out in the same tuberosities in the adult fish. The region round the fissure of the third ventricle would be the thalamus opticus; and the torus semicircularis I would, with some doubt, refer to the corpus geniculatum externum. FRITSCH has determined the deeper part of this torus as the corpus quadrigeminum, and the superficial part as the thalamus opticus. The interpretation of the latter may be partly correct, but the relation of the former to the aqueduct of Sylvius forms a valid objection to its homology as given by this author. Of the remaining parts of the brain to be considered, the passage extending from the base of the third ventricle to the pituitary body is easily recognised as the infundibulum, and the glandular body into which it enters is clearly the pituitary body. The relation of the former to the latter is another instance of a fœtal arrangement of higher animals, surviving as an adult arrangement in the lower. The hypoaria occupy strictly the position of the tuber cinereum, and the part called valvula cerebelli that of the valve of Wieussens, both being cases of structures better developed in animals of an inferior scale than in those of a superior. Finally, the cerebral lobes homologise the corpora striata, combined with the hemispheres of the brain; and although I have not discovered in the species examined by me the ventricles in those bodies described by WILDER (65), yet I do not doubt that in other species they may exist.

The presence of the fissure between the crura cerebri in the brain of fishes has some bearing on the theories lately propagated by SEMPER and DOHRN as to the origin of Vertebrata from the Annelida. The former author has not yet published any researches on the relation of the Vertebrate nervous system to that of the Invertebrata, but DOHRN (82) sees in the fissure belonging to the posterior end of the fourth Ventricle the remains of the space included in the commissures between the supra-œsophageal and infra-œsophageal ganglia of insects through which the œsophagus of the Invertebrate animal passes. There are several objections to this, one serious one being the amount of space to be filled up with nervous matter, of which no indications exist in the Teleostean brain. Mere likeness alone between the parts in the embryo fish and the insect would not suffice, as is shown by the curious resemblance between the cerebral cortex of a mouse and the tectum lobi optici of a Teleostean fish seen in a horizontal section, yet the optic lobes do not homologise the cerebral hemispheres. Another objection FRITSCH has pointed out is, that if the œsophagus passed through this point, the jaws and mouth would have been supplied by a trunk from the supra-œsophageal ganglion, the fifth nerve being in advance. But if the theory be true, some other foramen must be found (if the œsophagus when it disappeared left any trace of its former existence) through which it could have passed; such a foramen presents itself in the third ventricle, which, in conjunction with the infundibulum, forms an opening quite through the nervous tissue, being closed only below by the pituitary body and above by the pineal gland. The existence of the pituitary body has never been explained. A glandular structure developed from the mucous membrane of the throat attached to the brain, it seems quite out of place; but considered as the remains of a former œsophageal or pharyngeal gland its raison d'être seems accounted for. The epiphysis cerebri is more obscure, but appears to be the remains of some vascular body useful in an ancestral state of existence, for it certainly has no functions to perform in living species. I would submit, then, that if the œsophagus did once pass through the brain as in Invertebrata, it passed through the infundibulum and the third ventricle.

BIBLIOGRAPHY OF THE NERVOUS SYSTEM IN TELEOSTEI.

I have not been able to procure copies of books marked thus, *.

1. WILLIS, THOMÆ, Cerebri Anatome. 1664.
2. MALPIGHII, MARCELLI, De Cerebro epistolæ ad Carolum Fracassatum. 1664.
3. COLLINS, S., System of Comparative Anatomy. 1685.
4. HALLER, ALBERTI V., Opera Minora, tom. iii. 1768.
5. HALLER, A. VON, Elementa Physiologiæ corporis humani, tom. ii., p. 591.
6. VICQ D'AZYR, Mém. de Mathématique et de Physique, tom. vii. Paris, 1776.
7. CAMPER, P., Sämmtliche kleinere Schriften. Trans. into German by T. F. M. HERBELL. 1785.
8. MONRO, ALEX., Structure and Physiology of Fishes. 1785.
9. EBEL, GODOFREDI, Observationes Neurologicæ. 1788.
10. *SCARPA, ANTONIO, Disquisitiones Anatomicæ. 1789.
11. *CHAUSSIER, Exposition du Cerveau. 1807.
12. CARUS, CARL GUSTAV, Versuch einer Darstellung des Nervensystems, &c. 1814.
13. TREVIRANUS, G. R. and L. C., Vermischte Schriften, Anatomische, Bd. iii. 1816.
14. TIEDEMANN, F., Deutsches Archiv f. die Physiologie. Bd. ii. 1816.
15. TIEDEMANN, F., Anatomie und Bildungsgeschichte des Gehirns im Fœtus des Menschen. 1816.
16. ARSAKI, APOSTOLE, Commentatio de Piscium cerebro et Medulla Spinali. 1836.
17. WEBER, ERNESTO HENRICO, Anatomia conparata Nervi Sympathetici. 1817.
18. *WITTJACK, JOACH., De Piscium cerebro. Berolini, 1817.
19. ZAGORSKY, De Syst. Nerv. Piscium. 1833.
20. *WENZEL, De Penitiori Structurâ cerebri.
21. KUHL, HEINRICH, Beiträge zur Zoologie und vergleichenden Anatomie. 1820.
22. WEBER, ERNESTI HENRICI, De Aure et Auditu hominis et animalium. 1820.

23. BAILLY, E. M., Recherches d'Anatomie comparée du Système nerveux, &c.
    1823.

24. SOMMÉ, C. S. Recherches sur l'Anatomie comp. du Cerveau.   1824.

25. SERRES, E. R. A., Anatomie comparée du Cerveau.   1824.

26. DESMOULINS, A., Anatomie des Systèmes nerveux des Animaux vertébrés.
    1825.

27. WEBER, ERNST HEINRICH, Meckel's Archiv.   1827.

28. CUVIER et VALENCIENNES, Histoire Naturelle des Poissons.   1828.

29. TREVIRANUS, G. R., Über die hintern Hemisphären des Gehirns der Vögel, Am-
    phibien und Fische, Tiedemann und Treviranus Zeitschrift, Bd. iv.   1831.

30. GILTAY, CAROLI MARINI, Descriptio Neurologica Esocis Lucii.   Annales Acad.
    Lugduno Bataviæ, tom. xvii.   1833.

31. *STEIN, de Thalamo Optico et Origine N. Optici in homine et animalium.   1834.

32. BAER, KARL ERNST, v. Untersuchungen ü. d. Entwickelungsgeschichte der Fische.
    1835.—Also, Entwickelungsgeschichte der Thiere.   Zweiter Theil.

33. BÜCHNER, G., Mém. sur la Système nerveux du Barbeau (Cyprinus Barbus),
    Mém. de la Société d'Histoire Naturelle de Strasbourg, tom. ii.   1835.

34. GOTTSCHE, Müller's Archiv.   1835.

35. LEURET, FR., Anat. Comp. Système nerveux.   1839.

36. MÜLLER, JOHANNES, Vergleich. Anat. der Myxinoiden.   1840.

37. VOGT, C., Embryologie des Salmones in Hist. Naturelle des Poissons d'eau douce,
    par L. AGASSIZ.

38. STANNIUS, H., Peripherisches Nervensystem des Dorsch (Gadus callarias), Archiv
    für Anatomie.   1842.

39. GUILLOT, NATALIS, Exposition Anat. du centre nerveux, &c., Mém. Cour. de
    l'Acad. Royale de Bruxelles, tom. xvi.   1843.

40. *FLORMAN, ARVID, Recherches Struct. du Cerveau.   Paris, 1843.

41. *FOVILLE, Traité complet Anat. Syst. nerveux.   1844.

42. GIRGENSOHN, O. G. L., Anat. u. Phys. des Fisch-Nervensystems.   Mém. des
    Savants étrangers, St. Pétersbourg, tom. v.   1845.

43. STANNIUS, HERM., Das Peripherische Nervensystem der Fische.   1849.

44. KLAATSCH, H. M. A., de Cerebris Piscium.   1850.   Halis.

45. PHILIPEAUX ET VULPIAN, C. R., tom. xxxiv.

46. OWSJANNIKOW, PHILIPPUS, Disquisitiones Microscopicæ de Medullæ spinalis
    texturâ in Piscibus factitatæ.   1854.

47. ECKER, ALEX., Anat. Beschreib. des Gehirns vom Karpfenartigen Nilhecht.   1854.

48. KÖLLIKER, A., Zeitsch. f. Wissen. Zoologie, Bd. ix.   1857.

49. MAYER, F. J. C., Ueber den Bau des Gehirns der Fische.   Verhandl. der K. Leop.
    Car. Akad., Bd. xxx.   1859.

50. MAUTHNER, LUD., Untersuch. ü. d. Bau d. Rückenmarks der Fische.   Sitzber.
    d. K. Akad. der Wissensch., Bd. xxxiv.   Wien, 1859.

51. MARCUSEN, JOHANN, Die Familie Mormyren, Mém. de l'Acad. Imp. des Sciences de
    St. Pétersbourg, viiᵉ série, tom. vii. 1864.
52. DUMÉRIL, AUG., Hist. Naturelle des Poissons. 1864.
53. SWANN, JOSEPH, Illustrations of the Comparative Anatomy of the Nervous
    System. 1864.
54. BAUDELOT, Functions of the Encephalon of Fishes : Annales des Sciences Natu-
    relles. 1864.
55. HOLLARD, Comptes Rendus, tom. lx., p. 768. 1865.
56. VULPIAN, A., Leçons sur la Physiologie Générale et Comparée du Système
    nerveux. Paris, 1866.
57. OEFFINGER, H., Neue Untersuchungen ü. d. Bau des Gehirns vom Nilhecht.
    Archiv. f. Anatomie und Physiologie. 1867.
58. STIEDA, LUDWIG, Studien ü. das Central-Nervensystem der Knochenfische. Zeit.
    f. Wiss. Zool., Bd. xviii. 1868.—And published separately.
59. KUPFFER, Beob. ü. d. Entwick. der Knochenfische. Arch. f. Microscopische
    Anatomie, Bd. iv. 1868.
60. CLARKE, LOCKHART, Researches into the Intimate Structure of the Brain. Phil.
    Trans., Vol. 158. 1868.
61. BAUDELOT, Etude sur l'Anatomie Comparée de l'Encephale des Poissons. Mém.
    de la Société des Sc. Nat. de Strasbourg, Bd. vi. 1870.
62. MIKLUCHO-MACLAY, N. VON, Beiträge zur vergleichenden Neurologie der Wirbel-
    Thiere. Leipzig, 1870.
63. SCHAPRINGER, ALOIS, ü. d. Bildung des Medullarrohrs bei den Knochenfischen.
    Sitzber. d. K. Akad. der Wiss. Bd. lxiv. Wien, 1871.
64. STIEDA, L., ü. die Deutung der einzelnen Theile des Fischgehirns. Zeit. f. Wiss.
    Zool., Bd. xxiii. 1873.
65. WILDER, Professor BURT G., Proc. Acad. Nat. Science, Philadelphia. 1876.
66. FRITSCH, GUSTAV, Untersuchungen über den feineren Bau des Fischgehirns.
    Berlin, 1878.
67. GEGENBAUR, C., Grundriss der vergleichenden Anatomie. 1878.—And, Grundzüge
    der vergleichenden Anatomie. Leipzig, 1870.

List of Miscellaneous Works on the Nervous System referred to in this Paper.

68. STILLING, B., Ueber den Bau des Kleingehirns. 1846.
69. JACUBOWITSCH and OWSJANNIKOW, Microscopische Untersuchungen. Bull. Phys.
    Math. de l'Acad. de St. Pétersbourg, tom. xiv. 1854.
70. CLARKE, LOCKHART, Phil. Trans., Vols. 148, 149, and 152.
71. GERLACH, J., Microscopische Studien. 1858.
72. CLARKE, LOCKHART, Bau des Bulbus Olfactorius. Zeit. f. Wiss. Zool., Bd. xi. 1861.
73. DEITERS, OTTO, Untersuchungen ü. Gehirn u. Rückenmark. 1865.

74. JOLY, F., Zeit. f. Wiss. Zool. 1867.
75. KOSCHENIKOFF, Axencylinder-Vorsatz der Nervenzellen im Kleingehirn des Kalbes, Archiv f. Mikroscopische Anatomie, Bd. v. 1869.
76. HENLE, und MERKEL, Ü. die Bindesubstanz des Nervensystems. Zeit. f. Rationelle Medicin, Bd. xxxiv. 1870.
77. HADLICH, HEINRICH, Untersuchungen ü. das Kleingehirn. Archiv f. Mikroscopische Anat., Bd. vi. 1870.
78. OBERSTEINER, HEINRICH, Bau des Kleingehirns. Sitzb. der Wiener Akad., Bd. lx., Abth. ii., 1870; und Bd. lxi., Abth. i., 1870.
79. KOLLMANN, Sitzber. der Math. Phys. Klasse der Kais, Akad. der Wissench. München. 1872.
80. WEBE, MICH., Sitzber. der Akad. der Wiss. München. 1872.
81. MEYNERT, THEODOR, Stricker's Manual of Human and Comparative Histology, Sydenham Society, vol. ii. 1872.
82. DOHRN, Anton, der Ursprung der Wirbelthiere, &c. 1875.
83. SANKEY, H. R. D., Cerebellum, Quarterly Jour. of Microscopical Science, vol. xvi. 1876.
84. LEWISS, BEVAN, Lymph Spaces in Brain. Proc. Roy. Soc. 1877.

EXPLANATION OF PLATES.

The following letters have the same signification throughout :—

aq. Sy. Aqueduct of Sylvius.
a.v.c. Ala of the valve of the cerebellum.
c.a. Commissura ansulata.
c.c. Crura cerebri.
c.ca. Central canal of the spinal cord.
cbl. Cerebellum.
c.cbl. Crura cerebelli.
ce. Cerebral lobes.
c.l.c. Central longitudinal column.
c.l.o. Crura lobi optici.
c.pr. Commissura profunda.
d.c. Dorsal commissure of spinal cord.
d.h. Dorsal horn of grey matter.
d.r. Dorsal roots of spinal nerves.
ep. Ependyma.
fo. Fornix.

g.c.s. Ganglion cells of the substantia gelatinosa centralis.
gn.ab. Ganglion of the nervus abducens.
gn.mo. Ganglion of nervus motor oculi.
gn.tf. Ganglion of the trifacial.
gn.th. Ganglion of the thalamencephalon.
gn.v. Ganglion of the vagus.
hy. Hypoarium.
in. Infundibulum.
l.c. Lateral columns of the cord.
l.c. 5. Lower column of the trifacial.
l.op. Lobi optici.
m. Medulla.
m.f. Mauthner's fibres.
n. 1. Olfactory nerve.
n. 2. Optic nerve.
n. 3. Motores oculorum.
n. 4. Trochleares.
n. 5. Trifacial.
n. 6. Abducens.
n. 7. Facial.
n. 8. Acusticus.
n. 9. Glossopharyngeal.
n. 10. Vagus.
n. 11. First spinal nerve.
n.r. Nucleus rotundus.
ol. Olfactory lobe.
op.tr. Optic tract.
p.c. Posterior commissure.
pi. Pituitary body.
pr.c.t. Processus e cerebello ad testes.
p.m. Pia mater.
r.c. Restiform column.
s.g.c. Substantia gelatinosa centralis.
s.r. Fourth ventricle or sinus rhomboidalis.
s.v. saccus vasculosus.
t. Tectum lobi optici.
t.c.cbl. Transverse commissure of the cerebellum.
t.s. Torus semicircularis.
t.v. Tuberosity of the vagus.
u.c. 5. Upper column of the trifacial.
v.c. Valvula cerebelli.

v.h. Ventricle of the hypoarium.

v.h.g. Ventral horn of grey matter with ganglion cells.

v.l.c. Ventral longitudinal column.

v.op.l. Ventricle of the optic lobe.

v.pi. Ventricle of the pituitary body.

v.r. Ventral root of the spinal nerve.

v.t.c. Ventral transverse commissures of the medulla.

v.th. Third ventricle.

v.v.c. Ventricle of the valvula cerebelli.

Except when otherwise stated, all the illustrations are taken from specimens of
Mugil cephalus.

Fig. 1, Pl. 58. Longitudinal and vertical section through the brain of Grey Mullet (*Mugil cephalus*) made close to the mid-line. × 20.

Fig. 2, Pl. 58. Horizontal section through the brain of the Grey Mullet (*Mugil cephalus*) made on the level of the third ventricle. × 20.

Fig. 3, Pl. 59. Transverse section through the anterior end of the optic lobes, showing third ventricle. Infundibulum and pituitary body.

Fig. 4, Pl. 60. Transverse section through the optic lobe, valvula cerebelli and torus semicircularis, and anterior end of the aqueduct of Sylvius.

Fig. 5, Pl. 61. Transverse section through the origin of the nervus motor oculi and the commissura ansulata.

Fig. 6, Pl. 62. Transverse section through the trochlearis nerve. This section was composed from the inspection of several consecutive sections. It goes through the anterior end of the cerebellum and the posterior extremity of the optic lobe.

Fig. 7, Pl. 63. Transverse section through the anterior root of the trifacial.

Fig. 8, Pl. 64. Transverse section through the posterior end of the trifacial nerve, through the acusticus and through the abducens. This is taken from two or three contiguous sections of the same subject.

Fig. 9, Pl. 65. Transverse section through the narrow part of the fourth ventricle behind the crura cerebelli, through the anterior part of the ganglion of the vagus, and through the ganglion of the abducens. The fibres which eventually form the commissura ansulata first make their appearance in this section.

Fig. 10, Pl. 59. Transverse section through the posterior part of the fourth ventricle and the tuberosity and ganglion of the vagus.

Fig. 11, Pl. 60. Transverse section through the spinal cord immediately behind the fourth ventricle and through the posterior end of the ganglion of the vagus.

Fig. 12, Pl. 62. Transverse section through the spinal cord at the point where the dorsal root of the first spinal nerve emerges.

Fig. 13, Pl. 62. Transverse section through the spinal cord showing both dorsal and ventral roots of the first spinal nerve.

Fig. 14, Pl. 61. Transverse section through the spinal cord.

All sections from figs. 3 to 14, inclusive, are magnified 43 diameters.

Fig. 15, Pl. 63. Cells from the lobi olfactorii.

    a and *b*. Cells from the central group.

    c. A cell from the outer edge between the coarse neuroglia and the outer layer.

    d. Cell-like swelling from the outer layer of fibres.

    e.f. Tripolar cells from the inner edge of the outer layer of fibres. × 945.

Fig. 16, Pl. 63. *a* and *b*. Smaller cells near the external surface of the cerebral lobes.

    c. Cells from the central portion. *d*. A cell from the corona radiata. × 945.

Fig. 17, Pl. 63. Section through the superficial part of the cerebral lobes; showing the external layer of epithelium and the smaller cells.

Fig. 18, Pl. 64. Transverse section through the tectum lobi optici. × 170.

    a. An entering bundle of the crura lobi optici.

      1. External layer of granular matter.

      2. Obliquely directed coarse fibres with fusiform cells.

      3. Striated layer.

      4. Layer of inner obliquely-directed fibres.

      5. Transverse fibres of the crura lobi optici.

      6. Layer of minute cells.

      7. Ependyma.

    b. The most internal cells of the sixth layer, with the connective tissue attached.

    c. Deeper cells of the same layer.

    d. Fusiform cells of the second layer, with neuroglia attached.

Fig. 19, Pl. 64. Cells from the Fornix. × 945.

    a. Towards the proximal end.

    b. Towards the distal extremity.

Fig. 20, Pl. 64. *a*. Longitudinal section of the torus semicircularis of the Basse (*Labrax Lupus*). × 170.

    b. The superficial cells magnified. × 945.

    c. The larger cells, resembling those in the spinal cord.

    d. Sections of the crura lobi optici.

Fig. 21, Pl. 65. Cells from the hypoaria. All × 945.

    a. A cell from the general parenchyma.

    b. A group of cells from the neighbourhood of the ventricle of the hypoarium.

    c. Cells from beneath the epithelial lining of the infundibulum.

    d. Larger cells from the ventricle of the pituitary body.

Fig. 22, Pl. 65. *a.* Section of the nucleus rotundus of the hypoarium of *Crenilabrus.*

    a'a'. Placed opposite capillaries. × 61.

    b. One of the bodies in the nucleus rotundus of same specimen. × 565.

    b'b'. Placed opposite capillaries.

Fig. 23, Pls. 61 and 64. Longitudinal section of the cerebellum of the Grey Mullet.
    × 170, showing three of the layers which are found in that body.

Fig. 23. *a.* External layer of straight fibres.

    b. Second layer, consisting of cells of Purkinje.

    c. Third layer, consisting of minute cells.

    d. A Purkinje cell. × 565.

    e. Two minute cells from the third layer. × 945.

Fig. 24, Pl. 65. Longitudinal and vertical section through the brain of *Mugil,* taken more externally than fig. 1. Showing the commissures between the cerebellum, the optic lobe, and the hypoarium.

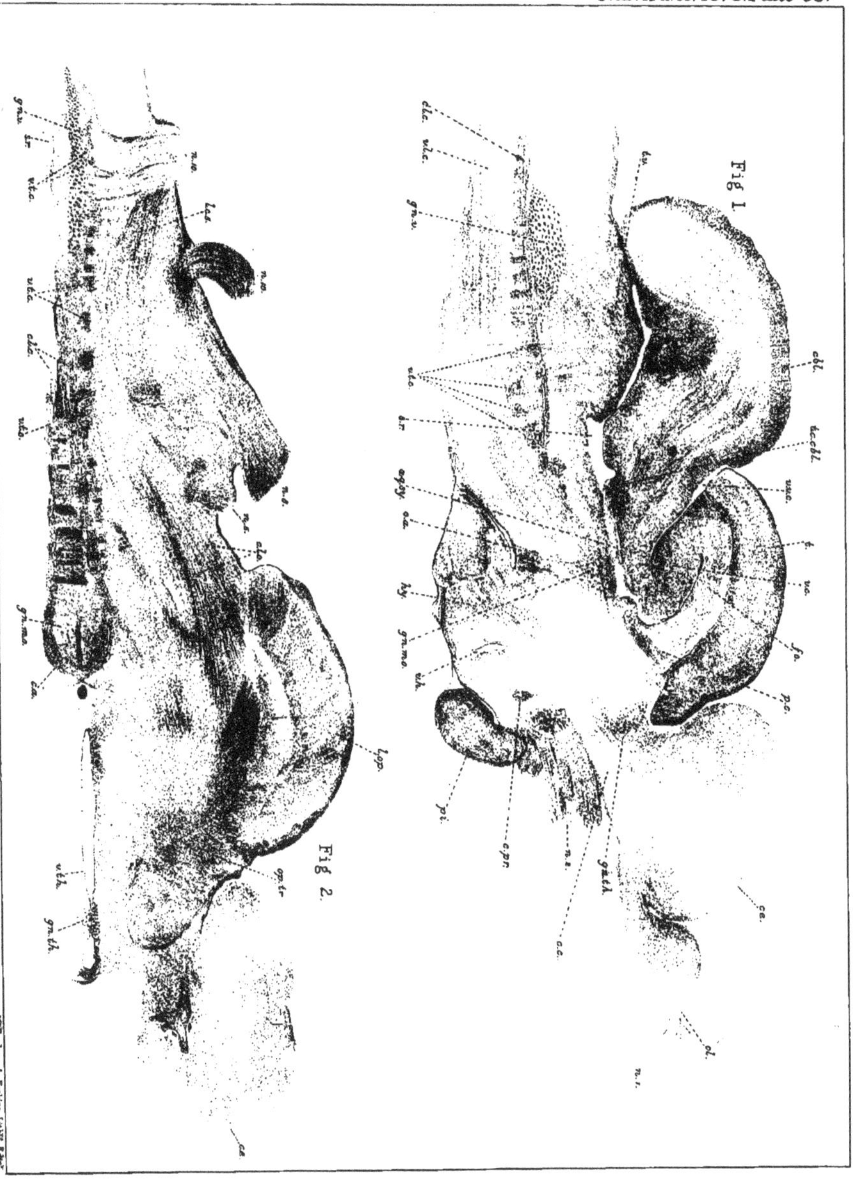

Fig 1.

Fig 2.

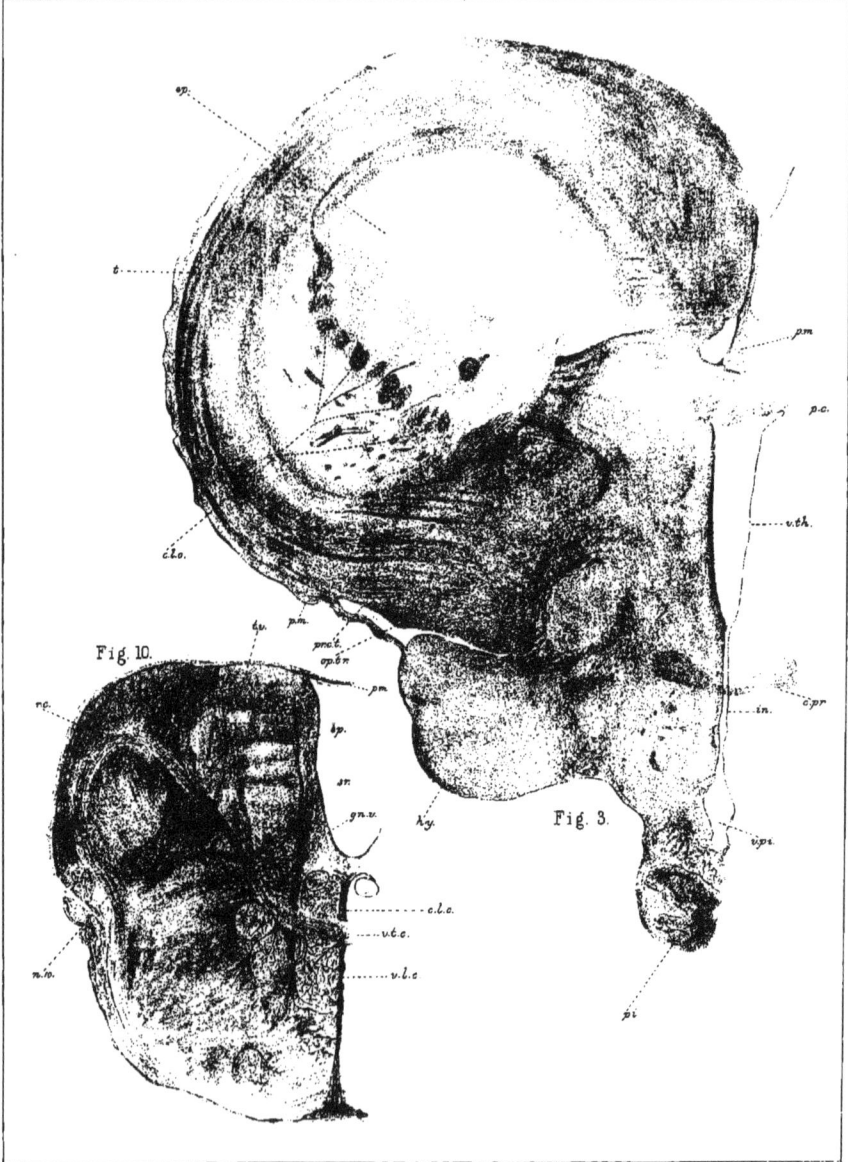

Fig. 10.

Fig. 3.

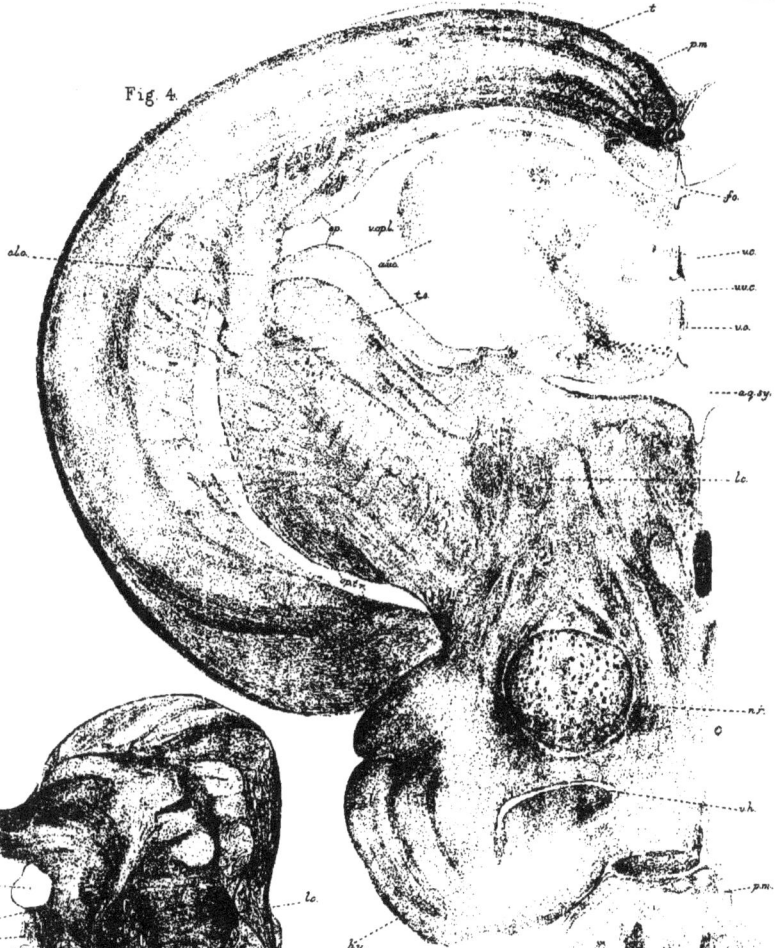

Fig 4.

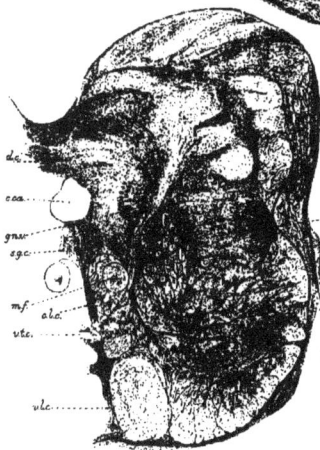

Fig 11.

McFarlane & Erskine, Lith!? Edin!

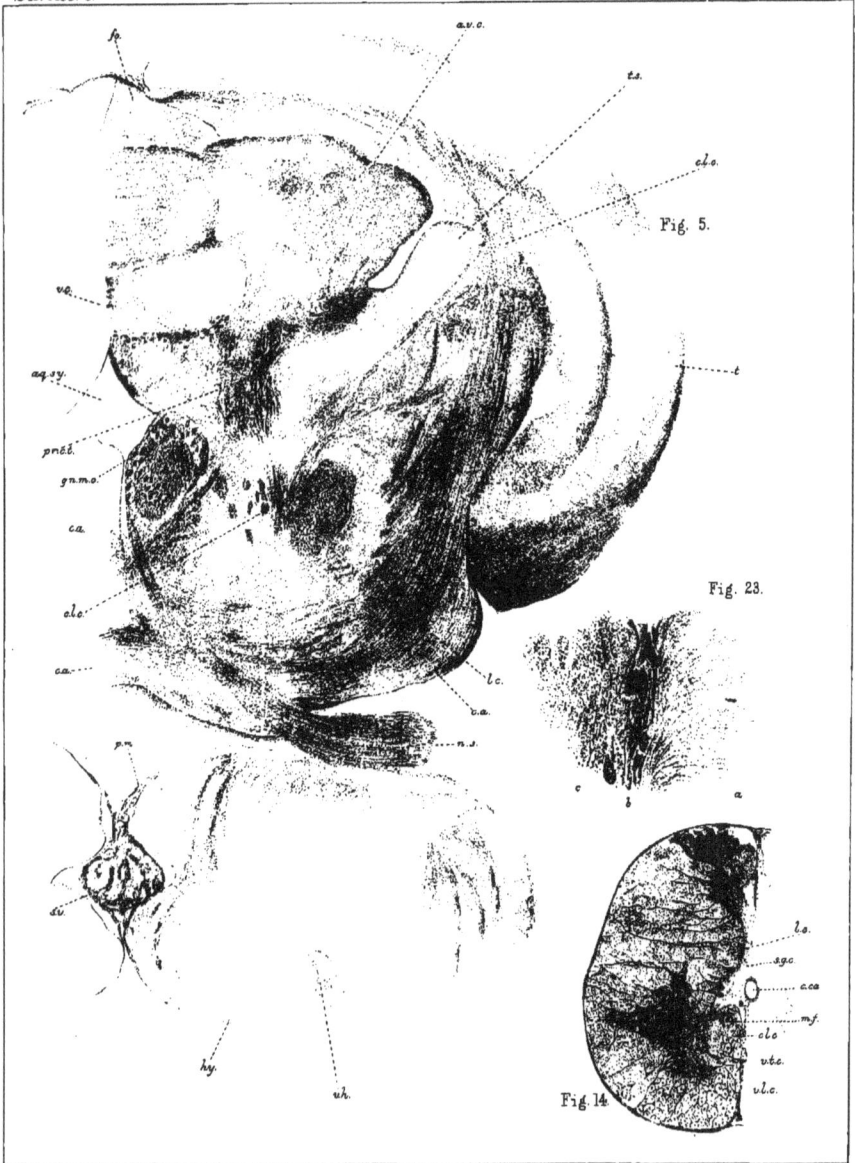

Fig. 5.

Fig. 23.

Fig. 14.

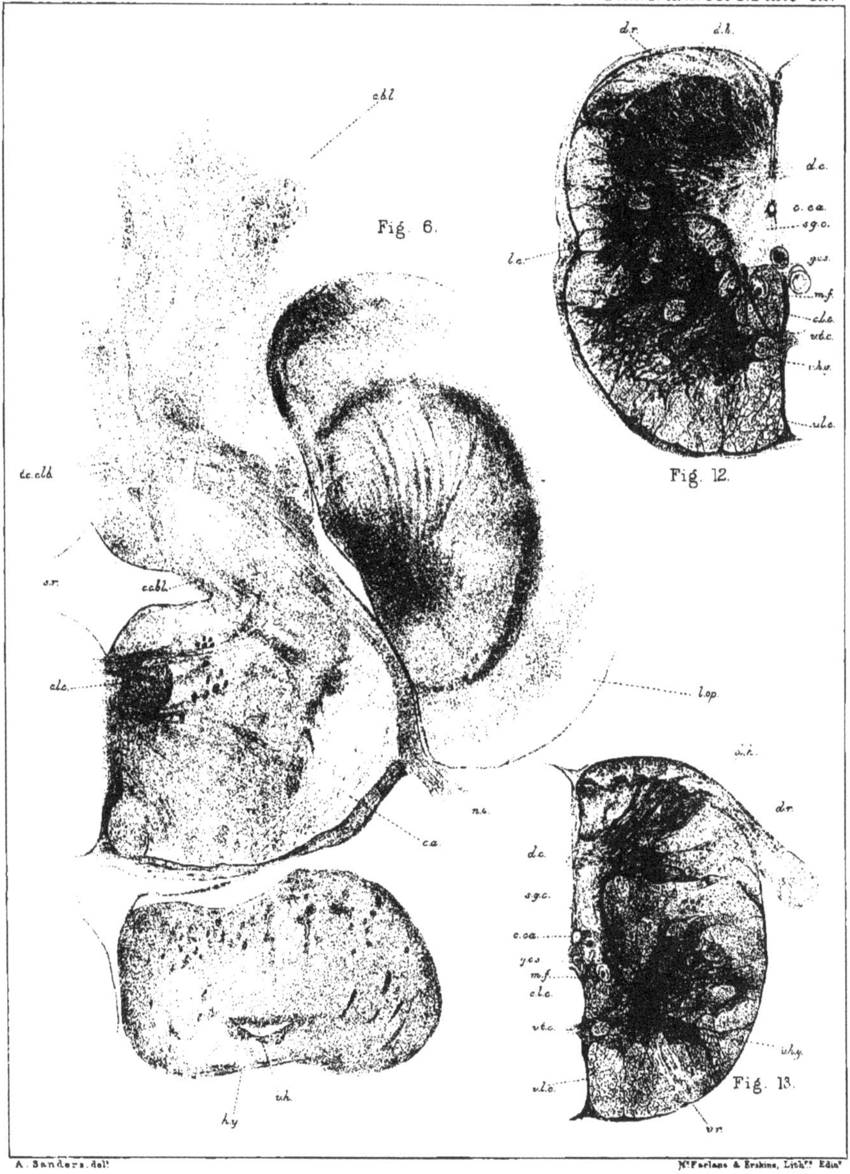

Fig. 6.

Fig. 12.

Fig. 13.

A. Sanders. del!   M?Farlane & Erskine, Lith?? Edin?

Fig 15.

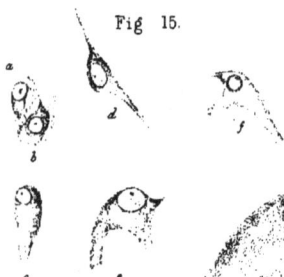

Fig 17.

Fig. 16.

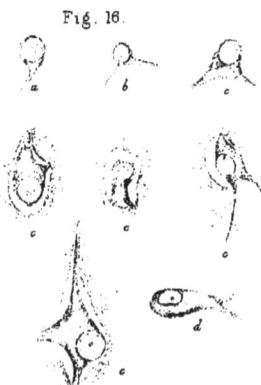

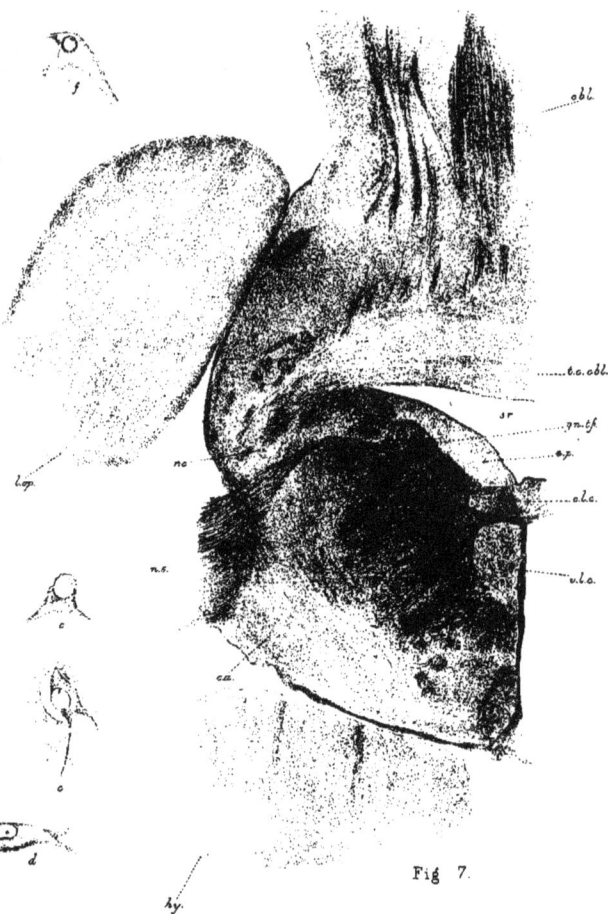

Fig 7.

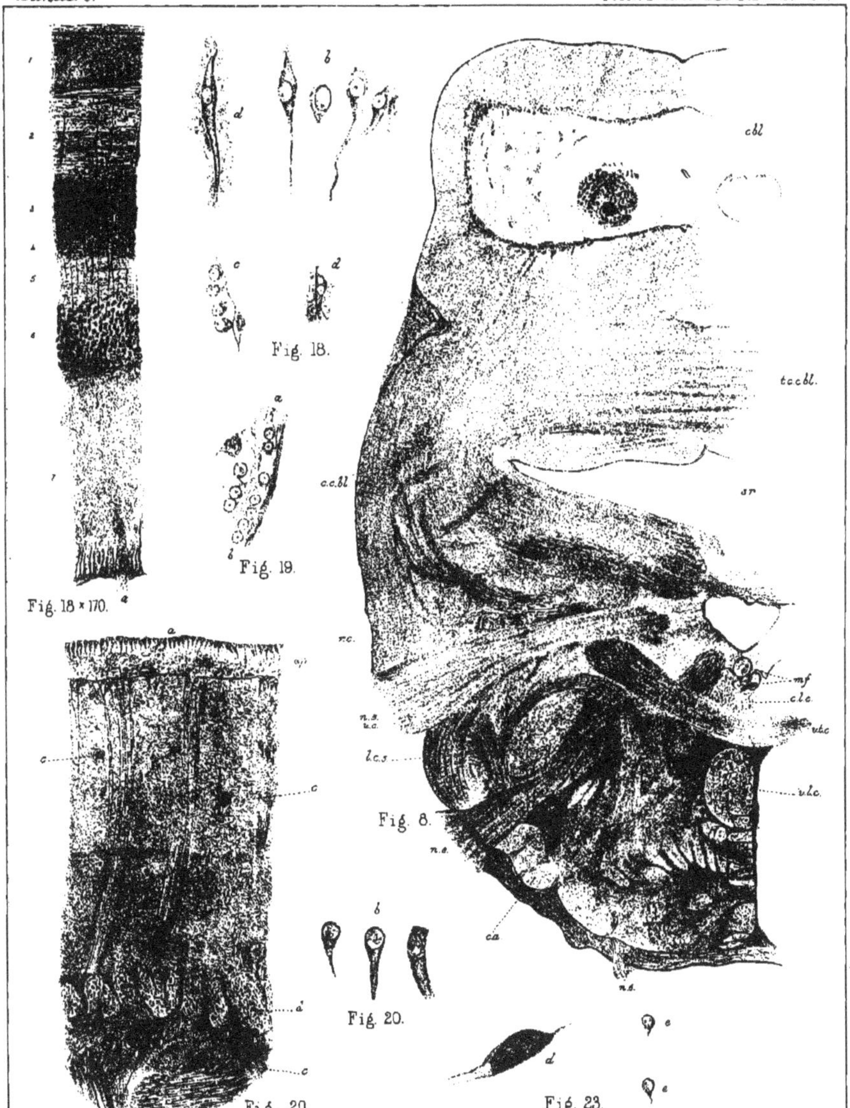
cbl
t.c.cbl.
c.c.bl
sr
r.c.
mf
c.l.c.
v.l.c.
l.c.s
n.e.
ca
Fig. 8.
Fig. 18.
Fig. 18 × 170.
Fig. 19.
Fig. 20.
Fig. 20.
Fig. 23.

A. Sanders, del.t McFarlane & Erskine, Lith.rs Edin.r

Fig. 9.

Fig. 22 a.

Fig. 22 a.

Fig. 22 b.

Fig. 21 a.

Fig. 21.

Fig. 24.